AF689687

A Century of Law at Notre Dame

Dean William Burns Lawless
University of Notre Dame Law School

A Century of Law at Notre Dame

Philip S. Moore, C.S.C.

UNIVERSITY OF NOTRE DAME PRESS
1969

Copyright ©
1970

University of Notre Dame Press
Notre Dame, Indiana 46556

Standard Book Number: 268-00416-1
Library of Congress Catalogue Card Number: 74-105724
Manufactured in the United States of America
by NAPCO Graphic Arts, Inc.

To

NOTRE DAME LAW STUDENTS AND LAWYERS:
PAST, PRESENT, FUTURE

FOREWORD

Ernest Hemingway once wrote to a friend that "If you are lucky enough to have lived in Paris as a young man, then wherever you go for the rest of your life, it stays with you, for Paris is a moveable feast." In much the same way over three thousand living American lawyers and judges have been at Notre Dame as young men and it stays with them because Notre Dame, too, is a "moveable feast." In the centennial year of the Law School, we record the highlights of the first one hundred years so that we understand better why this place "stays with us."

In December of 1968, on the eve of our Centennial Celebration, I asked Father Philip Moore to write our law school history. Not expecting he could possibly do it in less than a year, I was surprised when six months later he told me the work was done and he wished to discuss publication. This is typical of the author—direct, competent, he works seriously and straightaway.

Probably no person at Notre Dame has been in better position over the years to observe the law school's development. Most of his distinguished career as philosopher and historian have been spent at Notre Dame. As head of the Department of Philosophy, Dean of the Graduate School, Vice-President of Academic Affairs, and Assistant to the President, he has watched from a high perch overlooking the law school. He was a college student here during the last years of the first dean and he has known personally the men and the period of which he writes. He brings to the task the penetrating insights of the philosopher, the careful reporting of a medieval historian and the warmth of a true son of Notre Dame. Compassionate in his evaluation of deans and deeds, he presents a candid chronicle of the first one hundred years at the law school.

The school, as you will read, has had a long and difficult emergence. Unlike Notre Dame's athletic fortunes, the law school has not come to meteoric prominence with one "star" or with one "team." It has pursued a slow, plodding course upward, always upward.

We are indeed grateful that Philip Moore has been here to savor and write about our "moveable feast."

WILLIAM B. LAWLESS, *Dean*
Notre Dame Law School

Notre Dame, Indiana
July 24, 1969

ACKNOWLEDGEMENTS

In the pleasant task of writing this story of *A Century of Law at Notre Dame,* the author has had the generous cooperation and help of a number of persons. His thanks go first to the present Dean of the Law School, William B. Lawless, and to two former deans, Clarence E. Manion and Joseph O'Meara. Then he acknowledges his gratitude to the late Reverend Thomas T. McAvoy, C.S.C., University Archivist, until his untimely and unexpected death this past July 6, 1969, to the Reverend John E. Walsh, C.S.C., Vice-President for Academic Affairs at the university and his assistant, Mr. Leo Corbaci, to Professor Victor Schaeffer, Director of Special Collections at the university, to Mr. Stanley Farmann, Assistant Law Librarian, and to Mr. James Murphy, formerly Director of Public Information and now Assistant Vice-President for Public Relations, for their cooperation in placing at my disposal the several sources of this history which are in their respective charges. He is indebted to Mrs. Jeannette Allsop, former Executive Secretary of the Notre Dame Law Association, for detailed information on the association and its activities, to the Honorable Raymond Broderick,

Lieutenant Governor of Pennsylvania and former President of the Notre Dame Law Association for helpful suggestions, and to Mrs. Carol Berkowitz, secretary to Dean Lawless, for her courteous assistance. He extends thanks to Mr. Terrence O'Connor, second-year law student, who was his right-hand man in the collection of source materials, and to Mrs. Arabella Ellsworth and Miss Lorrie Gifford, who typed the manuscript. Special gratitude is extended to Professor James A. Corbett, who compiled the Index.

CONTENTS

1

The Early Years: 1869-1883

LIKE THE UNIVERSITY OF WHICH IT IS A PART, THE NOTRE Dame Law School of today had a humble and precarious beginning. Those who know the history of the university stand ever in awe before the bold venture of her founder, the Reverend Edward Sorin, and never cease to marvel that he and his collaborators, Brothers of the Congregation of the Holy Cross, were able to get underway a school, however nondescript, in primeval forest within two years of their setting foot on what today is the Notre Dame campus. But the energy of Sorin seems to have been unlimited, his faith deep, his thoughts big, his vision broad. Two years after the laying of the cornerstone of the first college building, now Old College, he obtained from the Legislature of the State of Indiana a charter in which his embryonic school bears the proud name of University of Notre Dame du Lac.

In view of this we are not unduly astonished when in the earliest extant printed catalogue Sorin expresses his intention of founding a Department of Law.[1] This was in 1854, and four years later courses in constitutional law were announced.[2] Ten years later, on October 5, 1968, the board of trustees decided on the establishment of a law department, and on February 1, 1869, the first law class was taught.[3] The establishment of the law department was "due to the perseverance and energy which have characterized the long and popular administration of Father Corby."[4] Two years earlier, on January 22, 1867, Timothy E. Howard, who for many years was to be a prominent member of the law faculty, wrote a letter to Father Sorin in which, after stating his qualifications for passing judgment, says that "as a college, Notre Dame is not successful." In his opinion, it was at best a prosperous high school.[5] If this evaluation is correct, we might conclude that the establishment of a law department was not only a bold undertaking, but even that it smacked of pretentiousness. This would be true were it not for the fact that in 1869 not even a high school diploma was required for entering upon the study of law for degree in most American law schools.

The first head, or principal, as he was called, of the law department was Professor M. P. Colovin. He disappears at the end of one year, and nothing is known of him except that he was the brother of the Reverend Patrick Colovin, fifth president of the university (1874–77). He was replaced by Professor Peter Foote, who is also on the university records for only one year. The only episode history seems to have recorded of him was his taking a few law students to Niles, Michigan, some ten miles distant, for a mild evening on the town at which "nothing was found wanting to satisfy the lawful aspirations of the excursionists," including a few toasts at the end of the dinner. But everyone was back on campus by seven-thirty that evening.[6] No one is named in the official catalogue as head of the law department from 1871 until William J. Hoynes was brought in as dean in 1883, although possibly Professor Lucius G. Tong gave it leadership, since he was the only member of the law faculty who gave continuous service during that period.[7]

In the early years of the law department, those entering it to work for a degree of bachelor of laws were required to have had "a good liberal education," although prospective students were informed that "those who have not completed their studies in the faculty of Arts will have the opportunity of doing so without extra charge while prosecuting their legal studies."[8] This requirement of a good liberal education for admittance to the study of law was higher than that at other schools. The *University Chronicle,* student paper at the University of Michigan, in its January 16, 1869, issue observed that it was agreeably surprised that Notre Dame demanded of its law students some previous education, and bemoaned that at Michigan law students had only to prove that they were eighteen years old and to present a certificate of good moral character.[9] However, Notre Dame soon reduced its admission requirement.

For many years the course leading to the degree of bachelor of laws was a two-year course. The subjects in the curriculum in the initial announcements were: First Year: Political Economy (Origin, Nature, and Division of Laws), Principles of Legislation, Introduction to the Study of Roman Law, Institutes of Justinian, Common Law of England, Public and Private Law, Principles of Obligation: how contracted, modified, interpreted and extinguished, Criminal Law and Procedure, and Medical Jurisprudence; Second Year: Constitutional Law of the United States, Principles of Civil Jurisprudence, as contained in the Pandects, Code and Novels, Jurisprudence of the United States, The Law of Contracts, Practice at Law and Equity, and The Law of Evidence. In addition to these regular courses, students were assisted in studying the laws peculiar to their respective states in preparation for their bar examinations. And finally they were given the opportunity to gain poise, self-command, and quickness of decision through participation in Moot Court, which soon became a weekly exercise. In addition to the classes and the moot court, a short essay on some legal matter they had studied was required of all students.[10] This seems to be a respectable program, although we may wonder how the small faculty of the time could teach it adequately.[11]

Changes in the originally announced program appeared in the very next year. Then in 1873–1874 and for the following ten years, courses were designated by the textbooks used: Wallace's *American Law,* Blackstone's *Commentaries,* Angell and Ames's *Corporations,* Kent's *Commentaries,* Parson's *Contracts,* Greenleaf's *Evidence,* Washburn's *Real Property,* Stephen's *Pleading,* Storey's *Conflict of Laws and Equity Jurisprudence,* and Bishop's *Criminal Law.*[12] No textbook was announced for Constitutional Law.

This designation of courses by textbooks used indicates that the study of these books, supplemented by lectures, was the primary method of instruction, giving the students a theoretical knowledge of the law; this method continues to be used. But a practical as well as a theoretical knowledge of legal matters was recognized as essential, so from the very outset the students were "required during the course to argue cases, draw up pleadings, and conduct Law and Chancery suits according to the rules and formalities of regular courts of justice."[13]

There is no record of the number of students the law department attracted in its initial years, but there must have been very few. At the end of two years, in June 1871, the degree of bachelor of laws was conferred on three men, James A. O'Reilly, Andrew J. O'Reilly and Lucius G. Tong. We have seen that Tong immediately joined the law faculty. This small number of graduates would indicate the small number of students enrolled in the department, but there is more explicit information. In a report on Notre Dame sent to the General Prefect of Studies of the Congregation of the Holy

Cross in 1872 by the Reverend August Lemonnier, fourth president of the university (1872–74), the prefect is informed that the law department has been discontinued. Father Lemonnier wrote:

> The Class of Law existed for two years and graduated a few students. Since 1870–71 [i.e., after the close of the school year 1870–71] it has ceased to exist for lack of students and professors. I am of the opinion that we are not old enough or patronized by the class of student that would support such a class and we had better discontinue it until better hopes can be entertained.[14]

In spite of this statement, the official catalogues reveal that the law department was dropped for only one year, 1871–1872, if at all. The only sign of a discontinuance is that no law degrees were conferred in 1872. But two degrees were conferred in 1873, one of which was on Timothy E. Howard, five in 1874, and by the end of the decade twenty-three lawyers held their degrees from Notre Dame. Therefore it seems evident that the decision of Father Lemonnier was quickly reversed, although it is equally evident that the reversal was not influenced by a significantly enlarged student enrollment, and effort was made to bring more law students to the university. An example of this effort appears in the *Annual Catalogue* of 1876–1877 (p. 30): "We trust to see our Law Department better, and better attended year after year. We have every reason to be proud of the young men who each year have sought the classic retirement of Notre Dame to pursue their Law Studies. We shall endeavor to make their sojourn among us an agreeable one and give them every facility for study." Judged by today's standards the facilities were minimal, but in historical perspective such a judgment is scarcely justified.

In the one hundred years of law at Notre Dame, many men have been on the law faculty, some of them outstanding jurists and professors. One of the earliest of them was Timothy E. Howard, who has already been mentioned. His was a long and prominent association with the university.

Timothy Howard first enrolled in 1859 as a sophomore, having completed his freshman year at the University of Michigan. In early 1862, after fulfilling the requirements for the bachelor of arts degree but before receiving it, he enlisted in the 12th Regiment of the Michigan Volunteers. Seriously wounded at the battle of Shiloh on April 6, 1862, he spent two months convalescing and was honorably discharged in June. He then returned to Notre Dame and received his bachelor's degree that same June. Two years later, in 1864, the university conferred on him the master of arts degree. The following fall he was appointed to the faculty as Professor of Rhetoric and English Literature.[15]

English literature was the field for which he was best prepared, but for the next few years he was assigned courses in several widely different subjects. This was common practice at the time, but Howard did not accept this fragmentation of his time and energy without protest. Thus, in the letter to Father Sorin in 1867 cited earlier, he complained that "professors are required to teach too many different branches, and, therefore, cannot teach any branch as well as they should." He himself "was trying to teach five different sciences —Astronomy, Rhetoric, Geometry and Trigonometry, Latin, and Conic Sections." He adduced such assignments of disparate classes as one reason why "as a college, Notre Dame is not successful" and added that "At Ann Arbor, the classes I teach would be distributed among at least four professors."[16]

What reaction this letter produced is a secret of history, but possibly there is some connection between it and the fact that in 1868 Howard was teaching in Northfield, Michigan, his hometown in 1859, when he first enrolled at Notre Dame. Be that as it may, he gladly accepted the university's invitation to return to Notre Dame for the second semester of the school year, 1868–1869.[17]

Perhaps his teaching load was reduced or at least limited in scope after his return. At any rate, he found time during the next few years to study law, and completed the course for his degree in 1873. Three years later, he joined the law faculty of which he remained a member until June 1916.[18]

Professor Howard's greatest academic contribution to Notre Dame was in law, but he also served the other divisions of the university—the Arts, Science, and Engineering. Because of his prominence on campus he was frequently called upon to welcome important visitors and to speak at public gatherings. In 1871 he was elected vice-president of the nascent Alumni Association.[19] When Notre Dame celebrated her Golden Jubilee in 1892, Howard was commissioned to write the history of the first fifty years; in his modesty, however, he withheld his name as author of the book.[20] The university has honored no other faculty member as she has honored Timothy Howard: in 1893 he was given an honorary doctor of laws degree; in 1898 he received the university's highest award, the Laetare Medal; and in 1924 a residence hall was named for him.

Professor Howard died on July 9, 1916, after a short illness. The *South Bend Tribune* of July 10 carried his obituary notice: "Few men have been so widely useful to the city, county, or state as Timothy Edward Howard and few have done so much so unselfishly and with so small profit to themselves. . . . He was in truth a many-sided man who as teacher, public official, expounder of the law, lawmaker, instructor of the law, as writer or speaker and as soldier, met the requirements put on him." He served the city and county as attorney from 1886 to 1892, and in 1909 he was elected councilman-at-large in South Bend. He also obtained the first park for the city, Howard Park. For the state, he was a member of the Indiana Senate from 1886 to 1892, and a Justice of the Supreme Court of Indiana–Chief Justice toward the end of his term, from 1893 to 1899. In 1899 he was president of the Indiana Fee and Salary Commission, and in 1903 was on the commission for revising and codifying the laws of Indiana. In addition in 1891 he was the author of an Indiana Tax Law.

The law department survived the early years, even though its situation never ceased to be precarious. The curriculum adequately covered the law as it was in the 1870s, but the method of teaching it, primarily through textbooks and lectures, was far from the best. Although there was some discussion of cases and practice in procedure in the moot court, no instruction in law through the rigorous use of the case method seems to have developed. The department was understaffed and the faculty could scarcely be called a strong one. The regular members who served through the 1870s were Lucius Tong, Francis Bigelow, and Timothy Howard. Howard was to become a distinguished jurist but had not yet achieved that stature during the 1870s.

Tong, also mentioned earlier, was first listed on the faculty of the university in 1864–1865. He was teaching bookkeeping and commercial law, and he helped set up the Commercial Course, from which the majority of Notre Dame students were then graduating. Concurrently he was studying law and in 1871 received his bachelor of laws degree; he immediately entered upon the teaching of law.

Bigelow received his bachelor of arts from Notre Dame in 1862 and the master's degree in 1867. Between these dates he worked in two law offices and in May 1865 was admitted to the practice of law before the Supreme Court of Michigan. He then read law in another law office in his hometown of Lancaster, Ohio, and in May 1866 was admitted to practice before the Supreme Court of Ohio.[21] He set up a law office in Dayton, Ohio, but he could not have practiced for more than a year or two, because in 1871 he is listed on the law faculty, and, moreover, he is a member of Holy Cross.

In the 1870s, law students were few in number and of indeterminate quality. The officers of the university must have been deeply concerned with this situation and most probably were aware of the dissatisfaction being voiced by the legal profession with the low quality of many graduates of American law schools. Then came the catastrophic fire which destroyed the second college building on April 23, 1879. There was no question that it had to be rebuilt and the work of the university continued. But what of the law department: should it be continued or dropped? The decision was a difficult one, but a dynamic new president, the Reverend Thomas E. Walsh, who became the sixth president in 1881, opted not only for the continuance but also for the strengthening of the department. To this end an alumnus, William J. Hoynes, was invited to head the law department, with title of dean.

NOTES

1. *University Catalogue* (1854–55), 6.
2. *University Annual Catalogue* (1858–59), 6.
3. Notre Dame *Scholastic,* II (1868–69), 47; [Timothy E. Howard], *A Brief History of the University of Notre Dame du Lac, Indiana, 1842–1892* (Chicago: The Warner Co., 1895), 122; *Annual Cat.* (1868–69), 19–21.
4. *Scholastic,* IV (1870–71), Dec. 31 issue, 7. Rev. William Corby, third president of Notre Dame.
5. Howard to Sorin, Jan. 22, 1867. Prov. Archives (Indiana).
6. *Scholastic* III (1869–70), 150. Cited in *Notre Dame: One Hundred Years* by Arthur J. Hope, C.S.C. (Notre Dame: University Press, revised edition, 1948), 152.

7. Lucius G. Tong appears for the first time in the list of faculty in the 1864–1865 school year. His subjects were bookkeeping and commercial law. He received the LL.B. in 1871 and was a member of the law faculty, 1871–72; 1873–82; 1892–98.
8. *Annual Cat.* (1868–69), 19.
9. *Scholastic,* II (1868–69), 159–160. Cited in Hope, *One Hundred Years,* 151.
10. *Annual Cat.* (1868–69), 19. In regard to moot court the statement reads: "For this end [to cultivate the art of public speaking] and in order to enable the students to acquire those habits of self-command and quickness of decision so characteristic of the learned and accomplished Lawyer, a moot court will be held from time to time under the direction of a professor, at which questions of law will be discussed and mock trials held."
11. In the first year, two men seem to have constituted the law faculty, Professors Colovin and Foote. During the 1870s a maximum of three men are named as regular faculty members; they were supplemented by several part-time members or lecturers.
12. Present-day students might stand aghast at the subject matter reported to have been covered by the examination in Criminal Law in June 1869: 1. The Criminal Law in General; 2. Military and Martial Law; 3. Jurisdiction over crimes with respect to their locality as between the United States and foreign nations; 4. Jurisdiction of the United States within and outside State limits; 5. Jurisdiction and local limits of the States; 6. Common law as a rule of decision; 7. Rules and principles of decision; 8. Intent; 9. Combinations of persons in the intent; 10. Necessity and compulsion; 11. Coverture; 12. Infancy; 13. Mental incapacity; 14. Corporations; 15. The Act; 16. Criminal and Civil

prosecution arising out of the same act; 17. Division of crimes; 18. Parties to a criminal transaction; 19. Compounding, misprison, and attempt; 20. Consequences which flow from crime. *Scholastic,* II (1868–69), 34.

13. *Ibid.,* 34.
14. Prov. Archives (Indiana).
15. Joseph A. Lyons, *Silver Jubilee of the University of Notre Dame* (Chicago: E. B. Myers and Co., Revised and enlarged, 1869), 113–115; Hope, *One Hundred Years,* 306–307.
16. Cf. *supra,* note 5.
17. Howard to Sorin, Nov. 10, 1868. Prov. Archives (Indiana).
18. From 1893 until 1903 Howard's name is not on the university Faculty list, but is listed on the law faculty for a course on the Appellate Jurisdiction of the Supreme Court. These years correspond with his term as judge on the Supreme Court of Indiana and with other political appointments.
19. Cf. Hope, *One Hundred Years,* 122, 155, 168, 179.
20. *A Brief History of the University of Notre Dame du Lac, Indiana, 1842–1892* (Chicago: The Warner Co., 1895).
21. Joseph A. Lyons, *Silver Jubilee,* 115–117.

2

The Hoynes Era 1883-1919

THE LETTER OF FATHER THOMAS WALSH TO WILLIAM Hoynes inviting him to become the head of the Notre Dame Law Department, with title of dean, and Hoynes's reply of acceptance have suffered the fate of countless historical records: they have been lost or destroyed. However, a brief note from Father Walsh, written after the appointment had been made, has survived. He wrote, "Classes will be resumed January 2nd. I need not tell you that there is a room here waiting for you and a hearty welcome besides, whenever you come."[1] And so Dean Hoynes arrived at Notre Dame in January

1883, and as dean and dean emeritus he was to remain until his death fifty years later, half the lifetime of the law school in this centennial year of 1969. During those fifty years he not only developed and strengthened what was then called the Law Department,[2] but also became perhaps the best known and best loved professor ever to serve on the faculty of the university. He was at once a strong personality, a master teacher, and a "character" whose little foibles and vanities charmed colleagues and students alike.

William J. Hoynes was born in Kilkenny, Ireland in 1846. Seven years later his parents emigrated to the United States and settled in LaCrosse, Wisconsin. In 1858, at age twelve, William quit school and became apprentice in a LaCrosse printing shop. Shortly after the outbreak of the Civil War he enlisted, at age fifteen, in the 20th Wisconsin Infantry. This was no wild, youthful adventure but an act of a deep and conscious patriotism which was to reveal itself in various ways throughout his life. Severely wounded at Prairie Grove, Arkansas in December 1862, he refused honorable discharge, fought through the battle of Vicksburg on July 4, 1863, and was finally mustered out in November 1863. Almost immediately he re-enlisted in the Second Wisconsin Cavalry, in which he served until the end of the war. This pertinacity was characteristic of his strong personality, and his years in army service also enkindled in him a lifelong love of the military.

After his return to civilian life, Hoynes went back to the printing trade and to three years of self-education.[3] But he soon realized the need for formal education and in 1868 he enrolled as a student at Notre Dame. He apparently spent one or two years here and then entered the University of Michigan Law School from which he received the bachelor of laws degree in 1872. He was admitted to the Michigan Bar in that same year, to practice before the Supreme Court of the United States in 1875 and before the Supreme Court of Illinois in 1877. He returned to Notre Dame to work for the master of arts degree which he received in 1878.

When he finished law at Michigan, young Hoynes wavered between journalism and law as choice of a professional career, and it seems that journalism might have been his choice had not Notre Dame offered him the position of dean of law in late 1882. From 1873 to 1878 he was editor of *The Daily Times* of New Brunswick, New Jersey; then he set up law practice in Chicago, but in 1881 he again went into journalism as editor of the *Daily Transcript* of Peoria, Illinois.[4]

Before recounting his work as dean for the next thirty-six years,[5] something should be said about two other facets of his rich, colorful personality—his posturing as an expert on things military and his involvement in matters political.

In reviewing his years of military service, it was remarked that "his years in army service . . . enkindled in him a lifelong love of the military." This love led him to make the study of military tactics and strategy a passionate hobby, and though there was much of pose and delightful vanity in this facet of his life, he did become very knowledgeable on the tactics of Civil War battles and the strategy of campaigns.[6] A most striking example of this posing is that to generations of students and to everybody else at Notre Dame he was known as "Colonel" Hoynes. The students, at least (among whom was the writer), who knew he had been a Union soldier, assumed that he had risen to this rank in military service, and the Colonel seldom bothered to correct this assumption. The young soldier had been mustered out of service as a private and the origin of his title had nothing to do with his valiant contribution to the victory of the North. Sometime in the 1880s he formed and drilled a company of student cadets which came to be called the Hoynes Light Guards, and it was these cadets who dubbed him "colonel," a title which became a term of affection. What few knew was that the colonel once became a general for a day. The occasion was a visit to Gettysburg in company with the Reverend James Burns, who later became ninth president of the university. As they toured the battlefield with other visitors, Hoynes described at length the course of the battle, with plentiful criticism of tactical mistakes on the field and strategic errors of those who had mapped the campaign, much to the awe of his audience. At the end of this harangue, Father Burns, who knew his companion's foibles and who was master of the subtle joke, introduced him to these listeners as "General Hoynes, late of the Union Army," and that gentleman is said to have accepted the new title without blinking an eye.[7]

The Hoynes papers in the University of Notre Dame Archives reveal that he was a powerful figure in Republican politics of St. Joseph County and the thirteenth congressional district of Indiana. In 1888 he was nominated to represent his district in the United States Congress. He was defeated, but only after he had waged a campaign which drew this praise in a *South Bend Tribune* editorial:

> The congressional canvas made by Colonel William Hoynes . . . was the most brilliant and aggressive ever known in this district. His campaign showed tact, brilliancy, courage, and above all it was clean. His line of battle was always formed on principles and never once descended to personalities. . . . The brilliant campaign of Colonel William Hoynes will not soon be forgotten.[8]

This ended his running for elective office, but not his political influence, which showed itself in numerous ways. Mention should be made of two important appointments he accepted. In 1890 President Benjamin Harrison appointed him to head a commission to negotiate with the Turtle Mountain Chippewa Indians on the delicate matter of moving from their lands in South Dakota to a reservation in Red Lake, Minnesota—a negotiation he carried out with eminent success.[9] In 1895 Governor Claude Matthews of Indiana appointed him to a commission, authorized by the 59th General Assembly, to plan the centennial celebration of the establishment of the Indiana Territory.[10]

In 1883, then, Dean Hoynes took over the direction of the Notre Dame Law School.[11] Excellence in any field of endeavor is in a sense relative, that is it must be judged in the context of time and circumstances. Thus, what was considered excellent a century or even fifty years ago might not be considered excellent today.

In this perspective, it can be said that during the long years of his tenure, Hoynes put the law school on a firm foundation and built it to an excellence of which we can still be proud. Graduates of the law school during Hoynes's last years as dean are still living, and are recognized to be fine lawyers.

Although Dean Hoynes arrived at Notre Dame in the midst of the school year 1882–1883, changes in the law program are announced in the *Annual Catalogue* of that year: "Numerous changes have been made in this Department. Chief among them may be mentioned the extending of the course to a period of three years, the raising of standards of studies to the most approved plane, and the partial substitution of the lecture system for the compulsory use of text-books . . ." The statement then announces that "It may now be confidently claimed that no law school in the country offers superior facilities for acquiring a thorough and practical knowledge of the law."[12]

Raising the standard of studies was of major importance. Two other important changes were the extension of the law course to three years and the "partial substitution of the lecture system for the compulsory use of text-books." This must mean that emphasis was shifted from textbooks to lectures in the method of instruction, because there had been some lecturing previously. This is borne out by the further remark that "the lectures are so full and comprehensive that they cover all subjects likely to arise in connection with even the most thorough examination." In the complete statement the students are advised to consult the standard textbooks, and then seemingly are told that the study of textbooks is superfluous, because by taking copious notes on the lectures they can acquire complete theoretical knowledge of the subject matter covered.[13]

The reason given for extending the law course from two to three years was recognition "that the standing of the profession had been lowered by a too indiscriminate admission to them [the law schools] of persons of limited education and technical education of a narrow and circumscribed range."[14] Although the additional year of law broadened the technical education, it is odd that, in view of the "limited education," the original requirement for entering upon the law, a "fairly liberal education" which in context had to mean some years of college work, was dropped. Not even a high school education was a strict requirement; the applicant had only to be seventeen years of age and to have had a fair English education. In 1889 the admission requirement was modified somewhat and the statement reads: "The regular course of study comprises three years. The student in it must be at least 17 years of age. He must have a fair general education and be able accurately to write the English language. A preliminary examination may be resorted to as a means of ascertaining his educational studies."[15] This minimal requirement perdured until 1917, when one year of college was added. This was increased to two years in 1926 and to three years in 1928. Also in 1889 the two-year course was revived and made alternate to the three-year course. The only variant in the admission requirement for the two-year course was that the student must be at least eighteen years of age. Then, what seems surprising, it is recommended "that only collegiate graduates should attempt the two-year program."[16]

To return to 1883, no definite program of courses by years is given. It is simply announced that the courses would cover the various branches of International, Constitutional, Commercial, Maritime and Criminal Law, together with Medical Jurisprudence, Common Law and Equity Pleading, Practice, Evidence, et cetera. The practice of law or practical law was still imparted through the moot court in which cases were tried once a week, the professor presiding as judge. This court was regularly organized, having its clerk, prosecuting attorney, sheriff, bailiff, reporters and other officers. Pleadings were prepared and filed, issues were joined, juries impaneled and cases tried in as close accordance as practicable with the procedures of regular county, state and federal courts. This functioning of the moot court continued pretty much unchanged down to the end of the Hoynes era.[17] Some changes in later years will be noted when we treat other eras in the history of law at Notre Dame. Worthy of attention here is that although some cases cited in the textbooks were analyzed and discussed in addition to the cases tried in the moot court, no strictly case method of instruction was employed in the 1880s.

It has been said that Dean Hoynes was a "one-man law school" during his first years at Notre Dame. This is an exaggeration, but throughout these years he did carry the brunt of the work, lecturing four periods a day and presiding over the moot court in addition to his administrative duties. Other faculty members during the 1880s and 1890s were Timothy Howard, A. C. Unsworth, John Gibbons, Andrew Egbert, John Ewing, Lucius Hubbard, Abraham Brick, William Breen, George Clarke and two or three lecturers. Nevertheless, by present-day standards, the law school was understaffed and the teachers overloaded.

The increase in enrollment was relatively rapid, due at least in part to the lowered admissions requirement, and averaged thirty-five to forty in the 1880s,[18] reaching up to seventy by 1900.[19] Few received degrees throughout the 1880s, the highest number being ten in 1889. From 1883 to 1886 inclusive there were only fifteen, and yet in the October 1886 issue the *Chicago Law Journal* paid Notre Dame the following tribute:

> Within the past three or four years the Law Department of the University of Notre Dame . . . has taken rank among the very best law schools in the country. Not one of its graduates during that time failed to pass a creditable examination for the Bar in any of the States. . . . It is worthy of note that the graduates of Notre Dame have not only passed the test in every case but also have, on several occasions, been highly complimented by the examiners.[20]

The twentieth year of law at Notre Dame was very important; it was a turning point, and several significant things happened during it and the year that followed. Before recounting these events, mention must be made of the first of what today are called "student activities,"[21] co-curricular activities not actually part of the regular program of studies but closely associated with it. Early in 1885 a Debating Society was formed and continued to function for many years. The *Scholastic* gave notice of its formation and purpose: "The Law Class has formed itself into a 'quizzing' club which meets regularly to discuss questions given in the lectures and such others as may be presented."[22] The questions debated were primarily legal questions but not limited to them. At a meeting in 1887 "The Debating Society considered the following question . . .: Resolved that clergymen are more beneficial to society than lawyers." The article continues, "Strange to say, the question was decided in favor of the negative. There must be something wrong with the Law Society."[23] Later in the same year the subject was "Protection versus Free Trade." The *Scholastic* observed that the Society "displayed good judgment by ignoring a long list of stereotyped subjects that usually catch the average debating society, and grappled with one of the questions of the day," which has a current ring to it, and concluded, "The debate was highly entertaining and thoroughly instructive, and we trust the example of the Society will be followed by our other societies."[24] We can presume that the debates continued to be both entertaining and instructive down through the years and added much to the formation of the young lawyers in poise and quick thinking in the heat of the argument.

In 1889 the official statement on admission requirements to the study of law were somewhat modified, although not greatly strengthened. In regard to the curriculum the *Annual Catalogue* of 1882–1883 listed no definite program of courses, but announced only the general areas covered, International, Constitutional, Commercial, Maritime and Criminal Law, et cetera; in 1889 the statement fails to mention even these general areas and reads simply: "These [the lectures] cover the whole domain of the law." On the other hand, the schedule of classes was given: three classes daily, two hours of lectures and one of quizzes and recitations, later increased to four classes daily, three hours of lectures and one of quizzes. Moreover, "Wednesday and Saturday evenings are devoted [respectively] to the Debating Society and Moot Court proceedings." The quizzes were said to be exceptionally instructive and interesting, designed "to make everything clear and intelligible." Finally, the thesis, required since 1884, was lengthened from thirty to forty folio pages.[25]

There is nothing remarkable in these changes, but a noteworthy change did occur: the case method of instruction was adopted. The students were drilled in both adjudicated and hypothetical cases. Today, the objective of such drill would be to sharpen the students' skill in analysis of legal matters; then it was to ground them in the principles of the law. The objective was to give students the answers—or at least the principles involved—to any and every question that could be legitimately asked in the bar examinations.[26] These principles were those of the Common Law; "the whole domain of the law" referred to above meant the Common Law. Statutes of individual states were excluded from all formal course work and the students were personally responsible for informing themselves on these.[27]

Adoption of the case method was an advance in the teaching of law, but how much it was used at first is impossible to determine. What seems to have happened was an evolutionary process in methodology with the case method finally becoming predominant. This conjecture is based on subsequent statements on the method of teaching law at Notre Dame. The first of these statements dates from 1895:

> The method of instruction may be called, for the sake of brevity, the eclectic system. It aims to combine the best features of the distinctive courses of other law schools, together with such additional and original means of imparting legal knowledge as to the Dean may seem proper. Two lectures are delivered daily, copious notes of which are taken by the students. They are also advised to read . . . the most important cases cited in the lectures. Instructive illustrations or actual cases, briefly stated, are given in explanation and support of such principles as may seem at all obscure to the learners. Text books on the subjects treated in the lectures are read collaterally by the students. The notes and text books are thus found to be reciprocally aidful and the principles are thus firmly fixed in the mind, as firmly as can be expected.[28]

A second statement occurs for 1898–1899, in which the method of instruction was explained at some length:

> Referring briefly to the prevailing methods of instruction in the different law schools, it may be stated that in some of them the text-book system is exclusively followed and the students read and recite daily an assigned lesson . . . ; in others the lecture system

> obtains, as in European universities, and students study notes to answer examination questions; in a few others, taking as guide a noted Eastern university, case reading is the favored system and students study books of selected cases . . . with a view to reciting them in outline or writing a brief digest of the points involved; in certain other schools an effort has been made to combine the distinctive features of case reading and text-book work or lecturing. . . . At Notre Dame none of these systems is exclusively followed. And yet the best features of all are comprised in the curriculum here preferred. It is believed, in short, that nowhere in the country is the course in law more comprehensive, thorough and practical than at this university.

The statement then continues:

> The lecture or dictation system alone may be pronounced antiquated and impractical . . . but in combination with text-book work, case reading and daily examination its great value and practical utility cannot be impugned. At Notre Dame it forms an important factor in the law curriculum. Each subject is fully covered by lectures, text-book work, daily and bi-monthly examinations, monthly theses, and the reading of pertinent cases and weekly trials in the Moot and other courts of the Law Department.[29]

One more statement on the methodology will suffice for the Hoynes era, that which appeared in the *University Bulletin*[30] for 1905–1906:

> The study of cases is usually begun in September and continues long enough to enable students to under-

> stand, analyze and criticize the decisions assigned to them for study and recitation. Lectures and explanations supplement this work. After thus familiarizing themselves with cases, they are expected to read the authorities cited daily in class, whether in the text books, lectures or quizzes. In the preparation also of theses from month to month . . . they must necessarily consult and cite them. In Moot Court work likewise, they are prepared for actual practice by making careful study not only of the cases in the reports but also of those cited in text books and digests.[31]

By 1905 the case method had won the day.

In 1890 a post-graduate course leading to the degree of master of laws was launched. The course required a year of study beyond the bachelor's degree, devoted to the work prescribed, the passing of examinations, and the writing of a thesis of forty folios on a legal topic selected by the student.[32] Although no specific courses are listed in the *Annual Catalogue* for that year, we can deduce from what is announced and from later listings of courses that for many years "the course of instruction" comprised practical exercises in the writing of pleadings, the examination of witnesses, the taking of depositions, the practical applications of the rules of evidence, preparation of briefs and arguments, the duties of certain persons, the examination of abstracts of title and the making of deeds, mortgages, leases, et cetera. Moot Court was also required.[33]

By 1904–1905 the course requirement for the degree of master of laws had changed considerably and included more substantive law: The State and Federal Courts and their Respective Functions, The Roman Law, The Law of Admiralty, Mines, Mining and Water Rights, Copyright, Patents and Trademarks, Trusts and Trustees, Interpretation and Construction of Statutes of State of Domicile and Federal Statutes, Powers and Functions of Masters-in-Chancery, Referees, Sheriffs, Coroners, Justices of the Peace, United States Commissioners, Arbitrators and Receivers.[34] After disappearing for a few years, the announcement of the "course of instruction" reappeared in the 1908–1909 *Bulletin* and continued to 1914–1915 in this form: "Graduate courses cover the entire field [of law] by way of review, together with Moot Court practice, office work, etc." Optional courses were made available in Roman Law, Admiralty, Mining and Water Rights, Copyrights, Patents, Trademarks, State and Federal Statutes.[35] If there was a rationale for these options and for the 1904–1905 program of courses, it is difficult to see. A complete change of program was introduced in 1915–1916, and courses for the master's degree were taken from Jurisprudence, Roman Law and Modern Codes, International Law, Admiralty, Administration Law, Legislative Bill Drafting, Statutory Construction, Medical Jurisprudence, General Review of Substantive Law and Procedure, and Practice in the University Courts.[36] The final change appeared in 1923–1924, when the course requirement was stated to be twenty-four semester hours in elective courses and in Anglo-American Legal History, History of European Law, and Modern Civil Law.[37] The master's degree program was dropped in 1928.

The inauguration of a program leading to the degree

of master of laws in the Notre Dame of 1890 might be considered somewhat adventuresome. The question arises, could there have been any connection between this and the providing of new, more spacious quarters for law the preceding year? In 1869 the nascent law department was housed in the third college building, erected in 1865. There was no place else to put it. No record remains of what space was allotted to it; perhaps a single classroom, at most two. Then came the fire of 1879 which destroyed this building, and when the decision was made to continue the law program despite this catastrophe, law was located in the new college building, the present administration building. Again, there is no record of the quarters it occupied. Whatever they may have been, they were, with a steady increase in students, cramped and overcrowded by the end of a decade. The entire university had become in need of more space, and these needs were met by the building in 1888–1889 of venerable Sorin Hall, the first private room residence facility at an American Catholic college. The south end of the first floor was to be the home of the law school for thirty years, and of Dean Hoynes until his death.

We have had occasion to remark earlier on the relativity of excellence considered as a subjective judgment of quality. This same relativity holds for physical facilities, which depends on a comparison, or contrast, of the new with the old. It is not surprising, therefore, that the new law quarters in Sorin Hall were described in glowing terms by contemporary writers. One description appeared in the *Columbia Law Times* for March

Sorin Hall

1889. The writer referred to the new building as a "magnificent structure" and continued, "The Moot Court library and lecture rooms are spacious, well lighted, well ventilated and exceptionally comfortable rooms and afford pleasant quarters for the students of the law course."[38]

Although the law quarters in Sorin Hall served their purpose for thirty years, they in turn became cramped and overcrowded and in June 1919 law moved to a new location, the first building of its own. It was erected in 1889 and named the Institute of Technology. Originally a three-story structure, it was "devoted to the exclusive use of the students of Civil, Mechanical and Electrical Engineering."[39] Later it housed the chemistry department. Then in September 1916 all but the outside walls was destroyed by a spectacular fire. This burned-out shell was converted into a two-story building as a new location for law. It provided several times more room than the quarters in Sorin Hall—a large courtroom, two large classrooms, a library and faculty offices—and it was hailed with great enthusiasm. The *University Bulletin* announcement of it reads:

> With the year 1919–1920 the College of Law of the University of Notre Dame began a new era. This year for the first time in the history of the school, the law men are afforded a distinctive law building all their own, and a law atmosphere separate and apart from the other schools and colleges. The splendid new and modern equipment and facilities lend dignity to the college, offer singular advantages to the law students and stimulates in them a zest for studying, under-

Hoynes College of Law

> standing and learning the law. Nowhere in the country are these conditions better. . . . The handsome building . . . is called the Hoynes College of Law. . . .[40]

And a later *Bulletin* states that "The courtroom is located on the first floor opposite the law library. In equipment, arrangement and compliance with the requisites of the actual court, it is superior to many real court chambers."[41] Hoynes's last act as dean was his participation in the dedication of this building named in his honor.

Library room is mentioned in the descriptions of both the Sorin Hall law quarters and the Hoynes College of Law. Looking back to the year 1869 and for many years thereafter we must wonder about the library materials available for the teaching of the bachelor of law program, and our wonder increases when we think of the master of laws course introduced in 1890. There is no mention of library in the *Annual Catalogue* for the early years nor mention elsewhere that has been found, but whatever library holdings there were must have been destroyed in the fire of 1879. The first mention found is in the history of the university written for the golden jubilee in 1892: "An excellent library comprising the standard text books and reports was purchased [sometime after Hoyne became dean], and was placed in the Moot Court, so as to be accessible to students at all reasonable hours."[42] The article in the *Columbia Law Times* cited in this history says, ". . . an excellent library comprising about twenty-five hundred volumes has been procured."[43] The next mention of the law library occurs in a special *Law Department*

Bulletin put out in 1904–1905, and its very smallness is said to be a possible advantage:

> There are undoubtedly in the country several law school libraries considerably larger than the library at Notre Dame, but it may well be questioned whether any of them shows more care in the choice of books or is better adapted for the use of students. All the latest reports of State and Federal courts are in its shelves, and no difficulty is experienced at any time in finding cases needed for reference, thesis writing, and Moot Court work. A great library, with crowdingly large attendance of students—too many to be personally known by or have personal attention from the Faculty—may be less available for use or accessible than a comparatively small one. The books used as the basis for recitation in class are chosen to a considerable extent from the Hornbook series. . . . As a rule, however, they are narrower than the range of study . . . [and] text books of merit are used outside that series.[44]

The *University Bulletin* of 1918–1919 (p. 125) states that the library contained more than five thousand volumes, "which are adequate for the present needs. . . ." In the *Bulletin* for the following year a more detailed statement on the library is published:

> The law library, quite extensive and adequate for the needs of our large and growing law school, is continually augmented by the arrival of new volumes. There are the U.S. Supreme Court Reports complete; Federal Cases; Federal Reporters; U.S. Statutes and Digests; Meyer's Federal Decisions; The National Re-

porter System, complete with Digests; Lawyers' Reports Annotated, both old and new series; American Reporter System, American Decisions, American Reports; American State Reports; English Ruling Cases; British Ruling Cases: American and English Annotated Cases; Moak's English Reports; Petersdorf Abridgement; American and English Corporation Cases; Moore's International Law Digest; American and English Encyclopedia of Law; Encyclopedias of Pleading and Practices of Evidence; Standard Encyclopedia of Pleading and Practice; hundreds of text books of the old and modern writers. There are the Indiana Supreme and Appellate Court Reports, complete; New York Common-law Reports; New York Court of Appeals Reports; Vermont Reports. There are now coming the state reports of Ohio, Illinois, Iowa, Michigan, Wisconsin, Minnesota, Pennsylvania, Massachusetts, Missouri, California and Connecticut. The library has a capacity of twenty thousand volumes, is admirably equipped . . . perfectly lighted . . . and like the court room and classrooms, is so arranged and cared for as to afford the most commodious, convenient and cheerful accomodations for efficient use.[45]

This was the library and its holdings at the end of the Hoynes era. In the statements cited, attention is called twice to the care given it, but there was no law librarian appointed until 1925.

We have noted what can be called definite stages in the development of law at Notre Dame—the early years from 1869 to 1883, and the periods from 1883 to 1889 and 1889 to 1898. A fourth stage began in 1898–1899, and a final one for the Hoynes era in 1904–1905. The principal delineator of each stage was the program of courses prescribed, although methods of instruction and other factors also played their roles. As in the past, one reason for the greatly revised program in 1898 was the dissatisfaction of the legal profession with the quality of those being admitted to the bar. Not a few schools were derelict in raising their standard of professional learning and ethics, and though Notre Dame was not to be numbered among these schools, the need was felt to restate her system of instruction, standard of proficiency and course of studies.

The period of study for the bachelor of laws degree was set at three years, as it had been in 1882, and the two-year course introduced as alternate in 1888 was dropped. The three years were designated Elementary, Junior and Senior. Students who had completed a collegiate course or who were judged to have achieved its equivalent through experience were eligible to enter immediately into the junior class.

In the elementary class only one daily hour of instruction was given, so that students whose general education was deficient could remedy their deficiency. This daily hour of instruction was based on the *Commentaries* of Blackstone and Kent, but other works on elementary law were also used: Walker's *American Law,* Smith's *Elementary Law,* Munson's *Elementary Practice,* Keener's *Selections on Jurisprudence,* Holland's *Elements of Jurisprudence* and Fishback's *Manual of Elementary Law.* If extensive assignments were given in these works, the students most likely considered one daily hour of instruction plenty.

In the junior year the prescribed courses were The Common and Statutory Laws, Persons and Domestic Relations, Contracts, Torts, Criminal Law and Procedure, Medical Jurisprudence, Common Law Pleadings, Code Pleading and Practice, Evidence, Sales, Insurance, Agency and Partnership; and in the Senior year, Equity Jurisprudence, Equity Pleadings and Practice, International Law, Constitutional Law, Private and Municipal Corporations, Personal Property and Real Property. We can agree with at least the first part of an evaluation statement that declared, "This course of instruction is comprehensive, thorough and practical. It is not and cannot be excelled."[46]

The next notable revision of the curriculum occurred in 1904–1905. The designations Elementary, Junior and Senior Classes were still used for the three years but they were also called First, Second and Third years. There were several changes in program: First Year: Personal Domestic Relations, Law of Contracts, Torts or Private Wrongs, Criminal Law or Public Wrongs, Forensic Medicine or Medical Jurisprudence and Toxicology, Property, Real and Personal; Second Year: Criminal Procedure, Corporations, Private and Public or Municipal, Partnership, Agency, Sales, Bailments and Carriers, Insurance: Fire, Life, Accident, Marine, Common Law Pleadings and Practice; Third Year: Equity Pleading and Practice, Code Pleading, Evidence, Damages, Bills, Notes and Checks, with Suretyship and Guaranty, Equity Jurisprudence, Wills, Executors and Administrators, Constitutional Law and International Law.[47]

The case method became the principal method of instruction around 1905 and remained so until the end of the Hoynes era, and the moot court also fulfilled substantially the same functions down through the years. The program of courses underwent almost continuous change, and one innovation occurred which was of great importance—the inauguration of the combination course. This course was first announced briefly in the *University Bulletin* for 1913–1914: "Students who desire can so arrange their studies as to complete any of the programs in the College of Arts and Letters and the Law program in six years. This will entitle them to two degrees."[48] This announcement was enlarged upon and the combination arrangement extended to the other colleges. Thus in the *University Bulletin* for 1921–1922, the statement, after pointing out that the better law schools of the country were beginning to require a bachelor's degree or at least three years of college work for admission to law, continued: "Although one year of college work suffices at present to admit a student to the College of Law as candidate for the degree of Bachelor of Laws, the law faculty, as well as the general faculty of the University, strongly urges upon the prospective law student that he pursue the six year program combining a course in the College of Arts and Letters, the College of Science or the College of Commerce with the course in law as candidate for two degrees, which otherwise required seven years of study."[49] The program provided that the bachelor's degree in any of the colleges be conferred at the end of the first year of law and the bachelor of laws at the end of the third. This combination course continued until its elimination in 1969, the only changes in it being the colleges with which the combination course was permitted, ranged back and forth from only the College of Arts and Letters to all four of the undergraduate colleges. It is impossible to say how many students availed themselves of the combination course in the years immediately following its introduction, but it seems reasonable to suppose that they were few until three years of college study was made mandatory for admission to the Law School in 1928. From that date until fairly recently the majority of law students at Notre Dame were following the combination program.

In the second decade of the twentieth century it was charged that law schools concentrated on teaching only the substantive law and failed to prepare students for the practice of law through treatment of the law of procedure. However, this charge did not apply to Notre Dame, where a thorough course in the law of procedure was given and plenty of practice provided, practice necessary for the development of the skills a courtroom lawyer must have.

This assertion that the Notre Dame Law School had not neglected to prepare students in practical law or the practice of law led the author of the announcement to list the university courts in which this practical education was given. The names and number of these courts had changed over the years[50] and in 1919–1920 were the Criminal Practice Court, the University Moot Court, the Notre Dame Circuit Court and the Supreme Court of Notre Dame.[51]

Until rather recently law students were not distinguished from undergraduate students in lists of students attending Notre Dame or in other statistical reports so it is impossible to state the annual increase in number of students in law. There were approximately seventy at the turn of the century and there was a steady increase in this number until the outbreak of World War I. In 1915–1916 the number was given as approximately two hundred.[52] A similar number is indicated in a letter of Francis J. Vurpillat, who was to replace William Hoynes as dean in 1919. In this letter Vurpillat says that there were ninety entering students in law in 1915 and that most of them enrolled for the second year in 1916.[53] The number of degrees conferred each year also gives some gauge of the total number of students. Thus there were thirteen bachelor of law degrees granted in 1900, and thirty-four in 1916. The outbreak of war in 1917 greatly reduced the number of students but it had built up again to well over two hundred by 1922.[54] Counted in these numbers were no doubt "special students" who were admitted to the law school for many years.[55]

As for the faculty from 1900 to 1919, the number varied from year to year and the turnover was great, as a brief study of Appendix IA will reveal. For some reason, the greatest number of both full-time and part-time members was highest from 1904 to 1907.

In bringing this chapter to a close, we return briefly to the man whose name it bears. After retiring from the office of dean and from the active faculty, Dean Emeritus Hoynes, who never married, continued to live in the Sorin Hall room into which he moved in 1889. He kept relatively active, writing legal and political articles, filling speaking engagements and carrying on a limited legal practice and heavy correspondence. Many of his visitors were former students who came to express their esteem and affection. Many too were the written expressions of these sentiments; representative of these is taken from a letter written by Terrence B. Cosgrove, one of the most distinguished of Notre Dame law alumni: "I entertain for you, Colonel, a feeling of pronounced esteem and admiration."[56]

Sorrow gripped the university community when his death was announced on March 28, 1933. Telegrams of condolence poured in and in a last tribute to their old teacher and beloved friend, law graduates came from near and far to attend his solemn military funeral.[57] The *Notre Dame Lawyer* obituary said in part: "The life story of Colonel Hoynes stands as both a challenge and an inspiration to every law student. It is a challenge in that the goal it sets is a lofty one; an inspiration because it points out how that goal can be attained."[58] And the *Scholastic* commented: "Continually for fifty years he was a familiar and beloved figure at the University of Notre Dame. Lawyer, educator, soldier and Catholic gentleman, his brilliant career was marked by toil, accomplishment and devoted service."[59] But it was for Father John W. Cavanaugh, president of the university for a long span of the Hoynes years, to sum up in the funeral eulogy the thoughts and feelings of those who had known and worked with him:

> He was widely and deeply learned in his ponderous, polysyllabic way. He was one of the great figures in

the long succession of Notre Dame professors. He bore his own great part in the making of our Alma Mater. Colonel Hoynes will be remembered in love and reverence on this campus until the last who knew him follow him to eternity. His life will be an example and inspiration for generations to come.[60]

NOTES

1. T. E. Walsh to Hoynes, December 23, 1882. UNDA, Hoynes Papers.
2. The name Law Department was used from 1869 until 1898 when it was changed to School of Law. Then in 1905 a second change of name to College of Law occurred, a name which lasted until 1955 when a third change brought the present name, the Law School. This present title, or law at Notre Dame, will be used except in quotations where College of Law occurs.
3. That he worked at self-education is the point of an anecdote related by the Rev. Thomas A. Lahey, C.S.C., *Colonel Hoynes of Notre Dame* (Notre Dame: Ave Maria Press, 1948), p. 36: Father John Zahm once remarked that the first time he saw Hoynes as a student, he was carrying a *Webster's Unabridged Dictionary* under his arm. In recalling this years later, Father John W. Cavanaugh said that he was still carrying the dictionary, but in his head, not under his arm.
4. For these biographical data, cf. *Who's Who in Jurisprudence,* 1928–1929.
5. Hoynes retired from the deanship of the law school in June 1919. His last official act was his part in the dedication of the Hoynes' College of Law. His fourteen years spent on campus as Dean Emeritus rounded out the fifty years mentioned earlier.

6. Hoynes received and accepted many invitations to talk on military matters. One such invitation came from the principal of a South Bend high school who asked him to lecture before the students on "An Army, Its Organization, Tactics and Strategy." Stuart McKibbin to Hoynes, October 1, 1894. UNDA, Hoynes Papers.
7. Lahey, *Colonel Hoynes,* 33–34.
8. *South Bend Tribune* Nov. 17, 1888, 4. Cited by *Scholastic* XXII (1888–89), 235.
9. *South Bend Tribune* Oct. 6, 1890, cited by *Scholastic* XXIV (1890–91), 93; Lahey, *Colonel Hoynes,* 20–21; Statement of Disbursing Account of Expenses of the Commission, Office of the Assistant Treasurer of the United States, March 31, 1891. UNDA, Hoynes Papers.
10. Claude Matthews, Governor of Indiana, and William D. Owen, Secretary of State, to Hoynes; October 7, 1895. UNDA, Hoynes Papers.
11. At the time of Hoynes' appointment, this tribute appeared in the *Chicago Evening Journal:* "The University [of Notre Dame] authorities are to be congratulated in their selection. Mr. Hoynes as a speaker, writer, thinker and lawyer has no superior of his own age in the Northwest." Cited by Lahey, *Colonel Hoynes,* 13.
12. *Annual Catalogue* (1882–83), 37.
13. For the complete statement of changes, etc., cf. *ibid.,* 37–40.
14. *Ibid.,* 40.
15. *Ibid.* (1889–90), 108. A reason, or perhaps better a rationalization, for the lowered admission requirements was given in a special *Law Department Bulletin* for 1904–05, 9–10. The requirement of some law schools that applicants have a college degree or at least have completed two years of college work excluded from the law many young men with bright minds and superior endowments who might outstrip those with more formal education. In view of this, Notre Dame

favored lower admission requirements, because "it is not disposed to shut its doors to honest worth and promising manhood, even though the general education of the applicant brings him only to the threshold of the collegiate courses."

16. *Annual Catalogue,* 109.
17. [Timothy E. Howard], *A Brief History of the University of Notre Dame du Lac, Indiana, 1842–1892* (Chicago: The Warner Co., 1895), 124–125. Cf. also the *Annual Catalogue* (1893–94), 70, and following years; *The University Bulletin* (1913–14), 110.
18. *A Brief History,* 123.
19. Hope, *One Hundred Years,* 271.
20. Cited by *A Brief History,* 123–124.
21. Recently the moot court has been included under student activities, but for many years it was a prescribed part of the legal curriculum; hence the Debating Society may rightly be called the *first* student activity.
22. *Scholastic,* XVIII (1884–85), 337. It was several years later that the Debating Society found mention in the *Annual Catalogue.*
23. *Scholastic,* XXI (1887–88), 204.
24. *Ibid.,* 509
25. *Annual Catalogue* (1889–90), 110–111.
26. *Ibid.,* 111.
27. *Ibid.,* 112.
28. *A Brief History,* 123.
29. *Annual Catalogue* (1898–99), 129–130; 132. The "other courts" in the 1890s were Court of Chancery, Probate Court, Justice's Court, University Court of Appeals, United States District Court and United States Commissioners' Court. Nothing is said about how often these courts functioned, but many of the cases selected for instruction may have been dealt with in them.
30. The title *Annual Catalogue* was changed to *University Bulletin* in 1904–05.

31. *University Bulletin* (1905–06), 86.
32. *Annual Catalogue* (1889–90), 114: "The writer is expected to read the thesis at a special meeting of the class and to defend the propositions set forth in it." It also had to be approved by the dean.
33. In the *Annual Catalogue* for 1898–99, 145–146, is found the following list of postgraduate courses: Study of Statutes and System of Pleading of home state; Practice in Taking Depositions, Frequent Participation in Moot Court Trials, Arguments on Motions for New Trials, Preparation of Bills, Exceptions, Briefs, Records, and Abstracts of Records in Appeals, Framing of Arguments for a Rehearing, Duties of Masters-in-Chancery, Referees and Arbitrators, Duties of Assignees, Receivers and Public Officers, Examination of Abstracts of Title, and the Making of Deeds, Mortgages, Leases, etc., Conveyancing, A Critical Study of Pleadings, with Reference to Forms and Substances, Jurisdiction of the Federal Courts, the Roman Law, Comparative Constitutional Law and Jurisprudence.
34. *University Bulletin* (1904–05), 28–33.
35. *Ibid.* (1908–09), 110.
36. *Ibid.* (1915–16), 116.
37. *Ibid.* (1923–24), 301.
38. Cited by *A Brief History,* 125.
39. *Annual Catalogue* (1889–90), 12.
40. *University Bulletin* (1919–20), 144.
41. *Ibid.* (1922–23), 289.
42. *A Brief History,* 123.
43. *Ibid.*, 125. The complete citation taken from the Columbia *Law Times* for March 1889 reads: "He [Dean Hoynes] introduced a system of instruction somewhat elective in its general features in that it combined the most approved methods of teaching followed in other schools. . . . The number of students has steadily increased. The average ratio of increase has been from

eight to ten a year. Professor Hoynes has labored so assiduously and effectively to promote the interests of the school that it now ranks favorably with the best law schools in the country. . . . studies have been raised to the highest and most approved plane and an excellent library comprising about 2,500 volumes has been procured."

44. *Law Department Bulletin* (1904–05), 38 and 40.
45. *University Bulletin* (1919–20), 144–145.
46. For the full announcement of the "course of instruction," cf. *Annual Catalogue* (1898–99), 127 ff.
47. *Law Department Bulletin* (1904–05), 15–28.
48. *University Bulletin* (1913–14), 107.
49. *Ibid.* (1921–22), 286–287.
50. Cf. *supra,* note 29.
51. *University Bulletin* (1919–20), 150–151.
52. *Ibid.* (1915–16), 106.
53. Vurpillat to Rev. James A. Burns, C.S.C., July 26, 1919. UNDA, Vurpillat Papers.
54. James A. Burns to Harry L. Thompson, May 21, 1922. UNDA. *University Bulletin* (1922–23), 287.
55. "Students who do not intend to become candidates for the degree of Bachelor of Laws, but wish simply to add to their educational acquirements a knowledge of the fundamental principles of law, may at any time in the year have their names enrolled on the list of special students." This announcement taken from the *University Bulletin* of 1914–15 is substantially the same as that published year after year.
56. Terrence B. Cosgrove to Hoynes, January 19, 1925. UNDA, Hoynes Papers.
57. Cf. Lahey, *Colonel Hoynes,* 83.
58. *Notre Dame Lawyer,* VIII (May, 1933), 391.
59. *Scholastic,* LXVI (1932–33), 6.
60. Cited by Lahey, *Colonel Hoynes,* 85.

3

The Vurpillat Era 1918-1923

THE NOTRE DAME LAW SCHOOL, DURING THE LONG tenure of William J. Hoynes, had taken rank among the better law schools of the country. But was there a sharp decline in its quality as well as in its size during the last years of this era? This question is raised by a letter written in 1918 by the man who was to succeed Hoynes as dean, Francis J. Vurpillat. With the outbreak of World War I, the number of students fell off sharply, but did the quality of the school go into an eclipse which would merit the severe charges lodged against it by the Vurpillat letter?

In this letter, addressed to Father John W. Cavanaugh, president of the university, Vurpillat states that he feels bound in duty to make known to the president his opinion on the state of the law school, and then lists his severe criticisms under five headings and adds a fact which he thought confirmed their validity. His first criticism was that the law course was treated "in its establishment, maintenance, conduct, methods of teaching and discipline, and standards of grading and graduation the same as the University treated the preparatory and common college courses." This, he asserted, was a basic error because "the law is a professional course, presumably a higher course, and should be regarded and treated accordingly. Law cannot be taught successfully in this manner and the result is that our Law School is discredited . . . by the University itself; is, therefore, not given such consideration and encouragement as it should receive; is generally regarded by the students and many of the faculty, clerical and lay, as an inferior Law School. . . ."

In his second criticism Vurpillat contended that "It is an impossibility . . . to conduct a Law School without an official, active, responsible head and a law organization, each respectively vested with the general jurisdiction . . . which can be exercised only by a lawyer and the law faculty . . . and yet, our Law School, the only one in the country to my knowledge, is actually trying to succeed without a law head or a law organization."

In his third criticism, Professor Vurpillat charged lack of uniformity in teaching methods and of co-ordination in the faculty. He asserted that "in the Law Department there must be uniformity in methods of teaching and discipline, in systems of class records, examinations and grading. . . . In this way alone can there be harmonious and concerted action by the faculty and uniform and satisfactory work by the students. In this way, too, will it be possible to secure such coordination in the faculty as will attain the highest efficiency in their work and the largest measure of success for the students."

The fourth indictment was leveled against the quality of the graduates. "The present system of grading and graduation of law students . . . is responsible for the conferring of law degrees . . . upon certain unqualified and incompetent men who soon appear before the bar examiners, make ignominious failures and reflect discredit upon the University." He continues, "Nor is it to the credit of the present system that the Law Department sends out many men of exceptional qualifications who do succeed, because this is accomplished in spite of these adverse conditions . . . and redounds solely to the efficient work of the professors and the ambition and earnest efforts of these students themselves." Interesting observations follow: "The law student is graded and graduated according to the general system applied in all the courses—a 70% passing grade . . . independently determined by the teacher of the respective classes. As each subject is passed . . . the next subject is taken up and passed in like manner until the final quarterly examination entitles the senior to his degree. . . . This system may be satisfactory for courses that are varied and independent subjects of study, but not so in the law course which presents but one subject, continuous, harmonious, dependent and entire—the law. Although of necessity divided into branches for logical treatment and taught by several professors, these classes and efforts must be co-ordinated and conducted under the supervision of the dean so as, in effect, to teach but one subject—the law."

The fifth criticism touches on the physical facilities which are declared wholly inadequate. "The present conditions and places afforded for teaching law are not conducive to creating the wholesome law atmosphere essential to classify the course and give it the special dignified character of a prominent professional course." The writer also found the library very inadequate in working space.

The sixth and final heading is not a criticism, but a fact confirming the validity of the criticism. He states that "our Law School is not recognized as of sufficient grade or standard to be entitled to admission to the Association of American Law Schools." Application for admission to the association had been turned down the previous year.[1]

What credence is to be given these criticisms and observations of Professor Vurpillat? Certainly, the criticisms are constructive and if the law school deserved them the situation must have been intolerable. The fact Vurpillat states to validate his criticisms cannot be gainsaid. The Notre Dame law school had not been admitted to membership in the Association of American Law Schools in 1918, and it would not be admitted until 1925, several years after the Vurpillat era. Then, the law quarters in Sorin Hall which had been spacious in 1889 when there were only about thirty-five students had become very inadequate thirty years later when there were some two hundred students. The over-crowded library must have been a particularly bad situation.

There was also ample reason for the first criticism. The law students were considered as just another group of college students, and even in the conduct of classes and grading, they were held to the same regulations as all other students. Their professional status was not properly recognized until many years later, a long time after the admission requirement was raised to include four years of collegiate study. At the time Professor Vurpillat wrote, law was simply one of the several colleges, and students entered upon its study as they did upon all other college courses, immediately after earning a high school certificate or the equivalent education.

Under the grading system and requirements for graduation fifty years ago, it was not only possible but even likely that degrees were conferred on some unqualified students in law and in other divisions of the university. Vurpillat was right in stating that a student could pass every class in his college course with a minimum passing grade of seventy percent and at the end be eligible for graduation. Only years later was a qualitative average considerably above the minimum passing grade for a class made a requirement for the receiving of a degree. Nevertheless, the writer conceded that there were many graduates with exceptional qualifications, most probably the majority, which in context indicates that students of quality and with strong motivation were among those admitted to the study of law. As for "ignominious failures" in the bar examinations, such failures probably were few. In the preceding chapter was noted the article in the *Chicago Law Journal* for October 1886 which highly commended the Notre Dame Law School for the success of its graduates in the bar examinations, and in a later chapter attention will be called to the generally successful record of law graduates in the bar examinations through the years.

There was basis in fact for some of Professor Vurpillat's criticisms of the Notre Dame Law School of 1918, but his charge that there was no "official, active, responsible head" of the law program is patently exaggerated. Dean Hoynes was still the official head and there is no reason to think that he had lost his sense of responsibility. It is credible, however, that failing health had slowed his activity and impaired his active direction, supervision and co-ordination of the law program. It was shortly after this charge was made, probably in the summer of 1918, that the decision was reached to retire him from the deanship. This decision may have been arrived at independently of the Vurpillat letter or it may have been influenced by it. The exaggeration in this charge is not easy to explain, and perhaps the ambition to succeed Hoynes as dean—ambition which was voiced in a subsequent letter—led Vurpillat subconsciously to overstate the facts and describe the law school, including its disorganization in teaching methods, as much worse than it actually was.

Father Cavanaugh did not answer this letter of criticism. At the time he received it, or shortly thereafter, he knew that he was about to enter on his last year as president of the university. He, therefore, filed it with the notation: "For the attention of my successor." He did, however, take two actions which may have been influenced to some extent at least by the letter: the retirement of Dean Hoynes and the decision to rebuild the fire-destroyed Chemistry Hall as a new and much more spacious home for the law school.

Father Cavanaugh's successor in the presidency was the Reverend James A. Burns, appointed in June 1919.[2] Professor Vurpillat lost no time in writing to Father Burns. In a letter dated July 26, 1919, he begins by a reference to his letter of March 11, 1918 to Father Cavanaugh. Then he goes on to say: "Some steps have been taken looking to the much needed reform of the Law School, notably the preparation and equipment of the splendid new law building." Nevertheless, the school was still very disorganized and "no catalogue can be published until it is re-organized and a plan for the future settled upon—what the Law School is to be and what it is to offer. . . . Many whose law education had been interrupted during the war would no doubt return, if they could be told plainly what courses would be offered and what their standing would be." He called attention to the reduction of the faculty to two members and stated that both men had too much to do. He wrote, "I am actually carrying the work that is usually assigned to three regular professors in the leading law schools of the country." Then he continued: "The re-organization of the Law School along lines of the modern law schools of the country, separating it from the common, everyday routine of the preparatory and common courses of the University, will necessitate change of policy at Notre Dame. At any rate, the Law School faculty must be provided, organized and directed, for at the present there is no faculty, no authorized head, and no system, methods or rules known to anybody." This brought him to his closing point, his own ambition to be named dean: "In this connection may I not state frankly my ambition and aspiration to be taken into the confidence of the University, proclaimed Dean of the Law School, assured an annual income for my services year after year for directing to the approval of the University a large modern Law School as well as teaching therein as at present."[3] Father Burns could find nothing to fault in Professor Vurpillat's ideas and ideals, and he appointed him dean of law sometime before the opening of the 1919–1920 school year.

Francis J. Vurpillat was born at Winamac, Indiana, in 1871. In June of 1891 he received his degree of bachelor of laws from Notre Dame.[4] On graduation he opened a law practice in his hometown and five years later was elected prosecuting attorney of Pulaski County on the Democratic ticket. He held this office until 1902. In 1908 he was again elected to public office and served as circuit judge of Pulaski and Starke counties until 1914. At the time of his election he was the youngest circuit judge in the State of Indiana; when he left the bench the Starke County *Democrat* paid him this tribute: "His record on the bench in this county during the past six years is . . ., we are pleased to [note], a credit to himself and to the people he served so well. The *Democrat* takes an honest pride in Judge Vurpillat's record. . . ."[5] He joined the law faculty of Notre Dame in 1915, and in 1919 was appointed dean, which position he held until the end of the 1922–1923 school year. He then went to Chicago as assistant corporation counsel to the city. He retained this post until 1933 when he was named attorney for the Federal Works Administration. In ill health, he retired in 1935 and returned to South Bend, where he made his home until his death on October 26, 1951.[6]

In the *University Bulletin* for 1920–1921 (p. 280), announcement was made that "with the school year 1919–1920 the College of Law began a new era, when a new and well-equipped building was provided for the exclusive use of the students of Law." This was no empty boast because the new building, the Hoynes College of Law, not only solved the serious problem of space but also stimulated the students in their application to study and gave them a greater sense of identity and independence. Thus one of them, writing in the first issue of the *Notre Dame Law Reporter* on the changes which had been initiated at the beginning of the 1919–1920 school year, asserted, "The scribes may recount the various forward steps that have been taken, but it were almost impossible to describe the new spirit that pervades the department, a spirit of proud contentment and achievement that is, it may be said, an inevitable accompaniment of the advance in legal paraphernalia and environment."[7]

The advent of a new dean was also reason for the sanguine announcement that the law school had entered upon a new era. The building had met one of the severe criticisms of the law situation which Professor Vurpillat had made in 1918, and as dean he moved to remedy other deficiencies to which he had called attention both in his letter to Father Cavanaugh and in his letter to Father Burns. Lack of supervision of classes and of leadership in co-ordinating the work of the faculty toward a coherent law course ranked high among these deficiencies. Hence the current *University Bulletin* stated: "The course is conducted under the careful supervision of the dean of the College to the end that the best methods may be applied and the highest degree of efficiency attained in the teaching department. . . ."[8]

Whether a higher quality student was admitted to the law school in the Vurpillat era is anybody's guess; it is certain that he did not get separate consideration for these students in regard to the grading system, regulations governing graduation, et cetera. Requirement for admission to law remained the same as it had been since 1917. In the *University Bulletin* for that year we read:

> Beginning in 1917 the Law Course will be a four year course. Students who have a bachelor's degree or who have completed at least one year of college can complete the Law Course in three years. Graduation from a four year high school or preparatory school of recognized standing, evidenced by certificate from such

> school, will admit one to the freshman class of the College of Law as a candidate for the degree of Bachelor of Laws. In the absence of such certificate, proof of established credits, a satisfactory examination based on the schedule of studies for entrance into the various colleges of the University is required.[9]

This tantalizing scope of the admission requirement had been characteristic for many years before 1917 and would remain so for some years after; every eventuality was covered lest some worthy but less educated applicant should be turned away. The student body increased rapidly and by 1922 reached nearly two hundred and fifty, larger than it had been before World War I.[10]

Like the admission requirement, the methods of instruction underwent no change under the new dean. They were based on the use of cases but care was taken to point out that "Excellent as the case method is for imparting a knowledge of the particular principles of the law applicable in the cases analyzed, a general idea of the law as a whole, its main features and universal concepts cannot be learned without the aid of the text-book. Therefore, the law is taught here by text-book assignments as well as cases, both explained and illustrated by the classroom talks of the instructors."[11] This statement was repeated for several years both before and after 1919–1920.

In his letter to Father Burns, Professor Vurpillat had written that a new *University Bulletin* could not be published until decision was made on what courses were to be offered the students. This implied that no specified schedule of courses had been announced in the immediately preceding *Bulletins,* but such schedules had been announced. In addition to the courses specified for each year of the three-year program, a special detailed notice was given on an Introduction to the Study of Law. This notice first appeared for 1917–1918. What is strange, in view of Vurpillat's letter, is that in the *University Bulletin* for 1919–1920 this notice is printed, but the schedule of specified courses is not given.[12] Explanation of this may be that Dean Vurpillat was not satisfied with the courses being offered and so omitted the schedule until he could revise it; a new program appeared the next year as follows: Sophomore Year: year courses in Contracts, Personal and Real Property, and Pleading, and semester courses in Torts, Sales, Criminal Law, Agency, Persons and Domestic Relations, and Criminal Practice Court. Junior Year: year courses in Property, Evidence, and Pleadings, and semester courses in Wills, Bills and Notes, Insurance, Damages, Quasi-Contracts, Briefing, Equity, Partnership, Suretyship, Mortgages, Trusts, and Notre Dame Circuit Court. Senior Year: year courses in Constitutional Law, Notre Dame Circuit Court, Supreme Court of Notre Dame and semester courses in Private Corporations, Administrative Law and Public Officers, Bankruptcy, Admiralty, International Law, The Conflict of Laws, Legal Ethics, Banks and Banking, Federal Income Tax, Water Rights and Mining Law.[13] It is not surprising that several of these courses carried only one semester hour of credit; this multiplicity of courses will be expanded upon later. To be noted here is the inclusion of Criminal Practice Court, Notre Dame Circuit Court and Supreme Court of Notre Dame in the schedule of courses. This was to give evidence that the charge brought against American law schools that they were failing to prepare students for the practice of law did not apply to the Notre Dame Law School.

In his letter of July 26, 1919 to Father Burns, Professor Vurpillat had written that the law faculty was reduced to two full-time members, who had far too much to do, and observed, "I am actually carrying the work that is usually assigned to three regular professors in the leading law schools of the country." Although this was a particularly sad state of affairs, it must be admitted that the law faculty was chronically understaffed and the members greatly overburdened. The wonder is that over the years it turned out the high-quality graduates it did. One of Dean Vurpillat's first tasks, therefore, was to rebuild the faculty. Judging from the records, he was able to recruit only one man, James P. Costello, for 1919–1920 and a second man, Edwin A. Frederickson, the following year. In 1921, however, he was more successful, and six full-time and three part-time faculty members are listed.[14] But it would still be a good many years before the law school would be properly staffed.

From Francis Vurpillat's letters to Fathers Cavanaugh and Burns in 1918 and 1919 respectively, before his appointment as dean, it is manifest that he rightly saw weaknesses or deficiencies in the law school, and there is evidence that as dean he tried to improve the prevailing conditions. However, most of his efforts failed and for reasons left unrecorded he was dismissed from office by Father Burns' successor in the presidency, Father Matthew Walsh, in July 1923.

The letter of Father Walsh in which he informed Dean Vurpillat of his dismissal is missing and we can only infer its contents from Vurpillat's reply: "The shock of the information that your Advisory Council has decided to depose and dismiss me has not abated." That he had not been told the reasons for the decision is plain from his attempt to conjecture what they could be. The possible reasons he thought were two, a controversy he had had with a faculty member, Professor Daniel Waters, and the displeasure of the Committee on Graduate Studies which he had incurred.[15]

The dispute with Waters arose over the latter's having barred from his class and from examinations two students without first consulting the dean, who contended that the teacher had overstepped his authority and insisted that the students be reinstated. The controversy must have become bitter, and the matter was referred to Father Walsh. This can be inferred from a letter sent the president by a Mr. Frank McDermitt, secretary of the Student Law Club." . . . Therefore we wish to be recorded as supporting to the fullest extent Judge Vurpillat in his present difficulty. It is our belief that he has been severely hampered in recent years by a lack of co-operation and confidence on the part of the University and the University Administration."[16]

In regard to the displeasure of the Committee on Graduate Studies, if it existed and was not merely presumed, it grew out of Dean Vurpillat's persistent efforts to have the University confer on him the degree of master of laws. He first broached this subject to Father Burns in a letter written a year after his appointment as dean, and he pushed the matter during the next year and a half. In his first letter he gave as reasons for his request his legal career, professional and public, over a period of thirty years, his attainments in the judiciary and his position as Dean of Law. He disclaimed personal ambition as his motivation and asked, "Would it not add prestige to the Law School and a more impressive appearance to the law bulletin if the dean were a master and not a mere bachelor of laws? And would it not be consistent with the contemplated [*sic*] course for the master's degree that the dean himself be a master?"[17]

This request was apparently referred to the committee on graduate studies, which rejected it. This rejection of his request must have been communicated to Dean Vurpillat, but the letter is missing, as may also be other correspondence. In any case, the next extant letter dates from more than a year later. In this letter Vurpillat appealed to Father Burns to reconsider the negative action that had been taken on his request.[18] This appeal was in turn denied, and he then took the rather drastic step of appealing to the board of trustees over the heads of both the committee and the president.[19] When this appeal failed, the unhappy dean apparently reconciled himself to a lost cause.

It is hardly probable that the reasons conjectured by Dean Vurpillat for his dismissal were the determining causes of the decision the university had reached in his regard, although they could have been part of a pattern of events which gradually led to dissatisfaction with his performance. In turn this dissatisfaction could have been the basis for the lack of confidence in the dean on the part of the university authorities, the lack of confidence sensed by the students in the Law Club and expressed in the resolution they sent to Father Walsh.

But whatever the reasons for Francis Vurpillat's being relieved of the office of dean and severed from the law faculty, the ending of this era in the history of the law school was hapless, even though the blow was softened by the university publicly accepting the dean's formal resignation.

NOTES

1. Francis J. Vurpillat to John W. Cavanaugh, C.S.C., March 11, 1918. UNDA, Vurpillat Papers.
2. Reverend James A. Burns, ninth president of Notre Dame, was the first university educated president. He held the doctor's degree in education. His short term of three years was among the most significant in the history of the university. He effected many important changes, one of which marked a turning point for the future of the school, the change from a high school-college institution to a college-university institution, the beginning of the "greater Notre Dame." Cf. Thomas T. McAvoy, C.S.C. "Notre Dame, 1919–1922; The Burns Revolution," *Review of Politics,* XXV, No. 4 (October, 1963), 431–450; Philip S. Moore, C.S.C., *Academic Development, University of Notre Dame: Past, Present and Future.* Mimeograph, 1960, 13–16.

3. Vurpillat to Burns, July 26, 1919. UNDA, Vurpillat Papers.
4. *Annual Catalogue* (1890–91), 102.
5. Cited by the *Scholastic,* XLVIII (1914–1915), 188.
6. *South Bend Tribune,* October 26, 1951.
7. *Notre Dame Law Reporter,* I, 1 (April, 1920), 57.
8. *University Bulletin* (1919–20), 147.
9. *Ibid.* (1917–18), 132–133; cf. also *ibid.* (1919–20), 151–52.
10. James A. Burns to Harry L. Thompson, May 21, 1922. UNDA, Vurpillat Papers.
11. *University Bulletin* (1919–20), 147.
12. This Introduction to the Study of Law was so comprehensive that it seems of interest to cite the content of this "course of preliminary lectures," which covered "The nature of law; law as it affects the individual; organized society and nations; the common law and equity systems, their origin, development and relations to the common law; the sources of the law, custom, judicial decisions and legislation; judicial systems and the processes of the courts, higher court decisions as precedents and the reporter system; the law divided into two great branches, the substantive law and the law of procedures—rights and remedies—and these laws again divided respectively into the law of contracts, wrongs, property and practice, pleading and evidence, these in turn divided into the special branches of the prescribed course; where to find the law; how to study the law." *University Bulletin* (1919–20), 148.
13. *Ibid.* (1920–21), 291–292.
14. In addition to Dean Vurpillat these members were Gallitzan Farabaugh, Edwin A. Frederickson, Arthur Hunter, John Tiernan and Daniel Waters, full-time; Stanislas Woywood, O.F.M., Vitus G. Jones and Samuel Parker, part-time.

15. Vurpillat to Walsh, July 8, 1923. UNDA, Vurpillat Papers.
16. McDermitt to Walsh, March 2, 1923. UNDA, Vurpillat Papers.
17. Vurpillat to Burns, July 20, 1920. UNDA, Vurpillat Papers.
18. Vurpillat to Burns, September 21, 1921. UNDA, Vurpillat Papers.
19. The record of this appeal to the trustees is in a letter of Vurpillat to Rev. William Cunningham, Chairman of the Committee on Graduate Studies, January 24, 1922. UNDA, Vurpillat Papers.

4

The Konop Era 1923-1941

THOMAS F. KONOP WAS THE MAN CHOSEN TO SUCCEED Dean Vurpillat in 1923. It is not difficult to imagine the task which faced the new dean. The law school was in considerable disarray and morale was at low ebb. That Dean Konop met the challenge with vigorous leadership is attested by a number of achievements from the very outset and confirmed by the admission of the Notre Dame Law School to membership in the Association of American Law Schools in 1925. Not long thereafter it received approved rating from the Council of Legal Education of the American Bar Association.[1]

Thomas F. Konop was born in Franklin, Wisconsin, in 1879. He attended college at the State Normal School at Oshkosh and graduated in 1900. He then began the study of law, taking his first year at the Illinois College of Law and the remainder at the University of Nebraska, from which he received the bachelor of laws in 1904. Somewhat remarkably, the month after taking his law degree, he was elected prosecuting attorney of Kewaunee County, in which office he served until 1910. With this taste of public service, he decided to run for the United States House of Representatives on the Democratic ticket. Successful in three campaigns, he represented the Ninth Congressional District of Wisconsin until 1917. Two years before leaving Congress he had joined in the establishment of a law partnership, Wigman, Konop, and Diener in Green Bay and there he began the practice of law at the end of his service in Washington. Later he became counsel to the Milwaukee Electric Company and the Wisconsin Gas and Electric Company, with an office in Milwaukee, and continued in this position until he was invited to become dean of law at Notre Dame. Testimony to his legal stature in Wisconsin was given by his appointment by a Republican administration to the State Industrial Commission shortly after his beginning practice in Green Bay. He also served for a number of years on the State Board of Vocational Education.[2]

As dean at Notre Dame, Konop kept up his interest in politics and the social movements of the day. He was chosen as one of fourteen law deans and professors to testify before the Senate Judiciary Committee on

President Roosevelt's proposal to reorganize the Supreme Court, the so-called court-packing proposal. He testified in support of the plan.[3] In 1941 Konop relinquished the office of dean, but remained active in teaching until 1949, at which date he retired to the small town of San Pierre, Indiana, where he died in 1964.

Entering upon his duties, Dean Konop immediately began to raise the requirements for admission to the Law School. In the *University Bulletin* for 1923–1924 (pp. 296–297) is the announcement: "With the beginning of the schoolyear September, 1925, only graduates of approved colleges and applicants who, in addition to a four year academic or high school course, have completed two years of work in an approved college will be admitted to the College of Law as candidate for degree. . . ." In 1928–1929 this was increased to three years of work in an approved college. Then in the *University Bulletin* for 1931–1932 (p. 7) a revised admission requirement announcement appeared: "The persons eligible for admission to regular standing in the College of Law are 1) graduates of a recognized college or university, and 2) those who have completed three years of work in the College of Arts and Letters, the College of Science, the College of Engineering, or the College of Commerce at the University of Notre Dame *or other college or university of approved standing, and have secured at least ninety semester hours of acceptable credit in college courses.*" (Emphasis added.) Nothing is expressly said about the combination course treated at some length in Chapter II, for students eligible for admission after three years of college work, for, although Notre Dame students took the combination course, students from other approved colleges and universities did not. Hence students with three years of successful college study were eligible for admission to the law school even though they were not following the combination course, and this would remain true until 1946–1947, when the words italicized in the above quotation were deleted from the announcement. Two years later schedules of specific courses in the combination program for Notre Dame undergraduates appeared for the first time.[4] For students not in a combination program, graduation from an approved college became mandatory only in 1946.

The case method had become well established as the primary method of instruction; the thorough and practical preparation of students for the practice of law continued to be the aim:

> It is the aim of the College to give its students a thorough and practical preparation for the practice of law in any state. The case method of instruction is used. By the study, comparison and discussion of selected cases, the principles of law are developed with reference both to their historical growth and to their application in contemporary practice. The classroom lectures and discussions are supplemented by collateral reading and by systematic training in the practice courts. In these practice courts, presided over by a Judge of the Superior Court of St. Joseph County, Indiana, the students receive training in the preparation of pleadings, motions, trial records, exceptions and appeals, and the preparation of cases for trial and briefs on appeal. Each candidate for a degree in

> law is required to conduct the complete procedure or at least one case from the service of process to final determination on appeal.[5]

In preceding chapters, programs of courses have been given in some detail for various years. The purposes of these listings have been to show what at different times the law faculty thought should go into the education of a lawyer and to reveal the gradual proliferation of courses in the program. All courses were prescribed, or required, and it seems that the aim was to cover almost every subject of substantive law and to give plenty of training in practical law. To achieve this, many courses were reduced to one semester hour of credit, which could give the students only a superficial knowledge of these subjects. Dean Konop apparently recognized this and his solution was the adoption of the elective system, although elective courses were never permitted first year law students. The *Bulletin* announcement of this important change reads:

> The curriculum has been recently revised. Since it is impossible for any student to obtain a complete mastery of the Law during the brief period of three years, the elective system has been in part adopted. Certain fundamental subjects are required of all. In addition to these required subjects the student, with the advice of the faculty may each year select other subjects with a view to preparing himself for a particular branch of the Law, or to meet the requirements of the profession in a particular state.[6]

In other words, the change in curriculum provided a basic education in law required of all students and the opportunity for each student to specialize in a branch of the law or even to merely prepare himself for bar examinations and practice in a particular state. This last provision strikes us today as an especially narrow notion of legal education; the provision for specialization on this level of legal education is a moot question. In this connection it is interesting to note here that at a later era of the law school the elective system was discarded for substantially the same reason as was given for its adoption.

In the first years following the adoption of the elective system, nineteen semester hours of electives were allowed, and, except for a short time around 1930, the number grew steadily until it was forty-six in 1950. In 1929–1930, when the elective hours were sixteen, the required courses were: First Year: year courses in Contracts, Torts, and Legal Responsibility, and semester courses in Agency, Bibliography, Common Law Actions, Pleadings, Criminal Law and Procedure, Personal Property and Bailments, and Real Property I: Rights in Land; Second Year: year course in Equity and Equity Pleading, and semester courses in Evidence, Procedure: Trial and Appellate, Real Property II: Titles and Wills, and Administration; Third Year: year courses in Constitutional Law, Court and Briefing, and semester courses in Private Corporations and Legal Ethics.[7]

This required program underwent some changes with the passing years, and it is of interest to record what it was in 1940–1941, the last year of the Konop era: First Year: year courses in Contracts, Torts and Legal Responsibility, Procedure I and II, and semester courses in Business Association, Bibliography, Criminal Law and Procedure, Personal Property and Bailments, and Domestic Relations; Second Year: year courses in Equity I and II, Evidence I and II, Real Property I and II; Third Year: semester courses in Conflict of Laws, Constitutional Law, Municipal Corporations, Private Corporations, and Practice Court and Briefing.[8]

Another innovation occurred in the program of studies for 1930–1931 and continued to be announced through the remainder of the Konop era. This was the Senior Seminars: "The senior class in the College of Law is divided into three seminar groups. These groups meet once a week for the purpose of discussing matters of practical importance. A member of the faculty presides at each meeting."[9] No elaboration or illustration is given of what the practical matters presented for discussion were.

We have noted that the student body in the law school was around two hundred and fifty when Thomas Konop became dean.[10] No records are available on student numbers for the Konop era, but they apparently declined greatly during the depression years of the 1930s, and had fallen to around fifty at the end of the decade.[11]

Although there is no information on the number of students for this era, there is much on the faculty. The new dean set himself at once to the building up of the teaching staff, and a special *College of Law Bulletin* for 1923–1924 (p. 17) announced: "With the opening of the schoolyear in 1923 the faculty was increased and strengthened by the addition of new members. At pres-

Present Law Building

ent five instructors are giving the whole time to the teaching of the Law and to the supervision of the work of the Law students. Then, others whose successful practice of the Law has won for them widely acknowledged leadership are engaged as regular lecturers." The aim of Dean Konop in the selection of staff was to form an integrated group of men possessing widely divergent qualifications. The constant turnover in staff probably defeated this objective during the 1920s, but in the 1930s a rather remarkable stability was maintained, at least among the full-time faculty members. These numbered six throughout the decade, with only one replacement, James J. Kearney for William Cain.[12]

The year 1930 was another milestone in the development of the physical facilities of the law school, as had been 1889 and 1919. In that year the construction of the present Law Building was completed in time for occupancy at the beginning of the school year. It was part of an extensive building program initiated by the Reverend Charles O'Donnell, eleventh president of the university. A gothic structure, its external iconography is the finest of the buildings at Notre Dame. Just as the Hoynes College of Law was spatially much superior to the old law quarters in Sorin Hall, so the new building was a great improvement over the Hoynes College of Law. The *Bulletin* description of it reads: "This [three-story] building, 157 feet long and 104 feet wide, has an assembly hall for 350 persons, four classrooms, four seminar rooms, a court room, a discussion room (which doubles as a student lounge), a library reading room 50 by 100 feet in which is a working library of 10,000 volumes . . . and additional stack room for 25,000 volumes, and offices for the dean, the librarian, the members of the faculty, and the *Notre Dame Lawyer.*"[13] This announcement continued year after year, only the estimated number of volumes in the library being a variant.

Magnificent as this new home was thought to be, it has long since been outgrown, and at present a new and far more spacious building is in the planning stage.

The inadequacy of the present law building for the needs of today is felt in several ways but it is truly crucial in regard to library space. The library is housed in a splendid, high-ceilinged room which might be easily renovated into a gothic chapel. But one cannot escape the suspicion that in designing it, the architect had in mind its esthetic quality rather than its function as a depository for books. There is much wasted space and no feasible way of transforming it into usable space. But in perspective one should not be too critical of the architect and of the others who were involved in planning the building; they probably never envisioned a time when library holdings would exceed or even reach the thirty-five-thousand-volumes stack capacity which they provided. The rate of growth of these holdings was painfully slow, and after sixty-one years of law at Notre Dame they numbered only ten thousand volumes in 1930. This number was to grow to sixteen thousand volumes by 1941, which represented an increase of twelve thousand volumes in the fifteen years from 1926 to 1941. The appointment of the first law librarian,

Mr. John Whitman, in 1925 may largely account for this relatively good showing.

Today the *Notre Dame Lawyer* holds high rank among the law periodicals edited and published by the students of American law schools. Its founding was a notable achievement of the Konop era, the first issue having appeared in November 1925. This issue makes no mention that the *Lawyer* had a predecessor, the *Notre Dame Law Reporter,* which has been largely unknown to succeeding generations of law students. This is understandable because its life span was only about eighteen months, April 1920 to November 1921, during which time seven issues were published, and the *Lawyer* is not a continuation of the *Reporter.* Despite its short life, a word should be said about this publication.

In the Foreword to the first issue it is stated that the *Reporter* would not be simply another law journal patterned on other law journals, of which there were enough, but would "constitute a new and novel departure in law school journalism." The "new and novel departure" is then spelled out: "The *Reporter,* which is to be published quarterly during the schoolyear, will be primarily a student publication, of and for and by the law student body. Its second feature, however, will be no less important than the first—that devoted to the interests of the law alumni. The purpose of these two departments in the *Reporter* is to bring together in fact as they are already united in spirit, the law school alumni and the law school students. . . ." In a word, those who founded the *Reporter* regarded it as a "family" periodical, a means of communication between alumni scattered abroad and students still "at home." Articles by jurists outside the family were, therefore, excluded from the purview of these founders. Although the *Reporter* was said to be a publication "of, for and by the law student body," its editor-in-chief was Dean Vurpillat, and its associate editors, the members of the faculty. Also there was a student staff of about twenty members, among the first of whom was a future dean of the law school, Clarence Manion.

To return to the *Notre Dame Lawyer,* the Foreword to the first issue is devoted entirely to the proud defense of the choice as motto for the new magazine, "Law is the perfection of human reason," maxim of Sir Edward Coke, the sixteenth- and seventeenth-century English jurist, in the face of current cynicism of those who no longer accorded the law "the venerable position enjoyed by it in the past." No trumpet is blown to announce that a new law periodical was being launched; no description of the character, purpose and scope of the "new magazine" is given. But the issue itself shows that the new publication was very much in the pattern of other American law school journals. It would be not only an organ through which the students could develop their writing and other legal skills but also another outlet for the studies of established jurists and lawyers in and out of the teaching profession. It would also be entirely student edited and managed; Mr. Clarence J. Ruddy was the first editor-in-chief; and Mr. Maurice Coughlin, the first business manager. Begun as a monthly journal in 1925, the *Lawyer* became a quarterly in 1930; in 1958, a fifth annual issue was added in which were published papers read at the law symposium held each year; and in 1962 this was increased to six issues.

As would be expected, the quality of the *Lawyer* has greatly improved over the years, but even the first volume is a creditable publication. Also the purpose and character of the review, unannounced at first, have later been defined in the official *Bulletins*. The earliest *Bulletin* statement reads: "The *Notre Dame Lawyer* is primarily a student publication. Its managerial and editorial staff is made up of students in the College of Law. Three members of the faculty act as faculty advisers. . . . It is published monthly during the scholastic year and contains articles by jurists, lawyers, and law professors, reviews of recent cases by students and also reviews of new publications."[14] This rather brief announcement continued throughout the Konop era, and was not elaborated upon until 1949–1950. The elaborated statement reads:

> The *Notre Dame Lawyer* was founded in the Fall of 1925. It appears quarterly, is wholly student edited, and reaches a large number of lawyers, public officials and scholars. . . . The quarterly brings to its readers lead articles by outstanding authorities in the legal profession, a book review section, a note section containing analyses of significant legal problems, and a section devoted to up-to-the-minute coverage of important recent decisions. The latter two sections are written by the student staff. The *Notre Dame Lawyer* aims, in the main, to fulfill the idea of a "Christian Law Review" and expresses the doctrines of the natural law.

> The quarterly is also intended to provide for its student staff excellent training in writing and in exhaustive legal research, which staff members are required to perform in preparation of notes and case work. Membership on the *Notre Dame Lawyer* is considered a distinct honor. Selection for staff members is based on (a) the student having a general scholastic average of 85% or higher; (b) his service for one year in the "In-Training" group; (c) his having had an article accepted for publication; and (d) approval of the dean upon recommendation by the editor.[15]

In the *Bulletin of the Law School* for 1969–1970 (p. 13), this announcement has been modified to read:

> The *Notre Dame Lawyer,* founded in 1925, is regularly published six times a year by students of the Notre Dame Law School. It affords qualified students an invaluable opportunity for training in precise analysis of legal problems and in clear and cogent presentation of legal issues. The *Lawyer* contains articles and book reviews by eminent members of the legal profession as well as comments and notes by members of the staff. The *Lawyer* is entirely student-edited and its integral and important part of the School's instructional program derives in large measure from this fact.
>
> Members of the staff are selected at the end of the first year of study on the basis of academic standing and appointment is recognized as a distinct honor.
>
> The Editor of the *Lawyer* is elected by the staff from the senior members on the basis of scholastic, literary and leadership achievements. He in turn selects the other officers.

In the preceding chapter was cited a letter from Frank McDermitt to Father Matthew Walsh in support of Dean Vurpillat in his controversy with a member of the law faculty. The letter conveyed to Father Walsh a resolution unanimously adopted by the Student Law Club and is dated March 2, 1923. Obviously, then, the club had been formed sometime before that date but for some reason did not receive recognition in the *University Bulletin* until 1928. Possibly it had lapsed for a time and was revived in 1928, but more probably it had been formed originally by the students as a private organization whose purpose was to manage social and other extra-curricular affairs; only later did it become a co-curricular activity. The first announcement of it reads: "The Law Club is primarily a student organization. It has charge of the extra-curricular activities of the College of Law. Lectures by prominent Judges and Members of the Bar are arranged for and delivered under its auspices."[16] The co-curricular activities increased with the passing years. Thus the announcement for 1942–1943 adds to that of the year 1928–1929, "The South Bend Committee of the American Bar Association holds meetings every month with senior members of the Law Club at the courthouse of St. Joseph County. At these meetings court dockets are examined and explained, and the mechanical features and routine operations incidental to the trial of lawsuits, probate of estates, the recording of instruments, execution of sales, and the like, are illustrated by court and county officials by references to actual public records."[17]

In 1950 the name was changed to the Student Law

Association and among the activities under its auspices were listed "the Natural Law Institute, the Law Ball, the Student Natural Law Debates, the Practicing Law Institute, the Senior Banquet, the Moot Court Competition and the Spring Dance. . . ."[18] In 1967 the name of the organization was again changed to the Student Bar Association; its purposes and functions had also changed considerably. The latest *Bulletin of the Law School* announces: "All students are eligible for membership in the Student Bar Association. The purpose of the Association is to foster the professional development and the social life of the students, and to represent their interests. It is a member of the American Law Student Association, which is sponsored by the American Bar Association.[19] The Student Bar Association has many important functions, including responsibility for administering the School's system of unproctored examinations, commonly known as The Honor System."[20]

At the time the law club first received recognition in the *University Bulletin,* the "Eleven" Clubs were also announced. These clubs were for members of the freshman class, who were subdivided into groups of eleven. Each group met weekly and at each meeting every member was required to give an impromptu talk. Twice each semester a convention of these clubs was held for parliamentary drill and an instruction on parliamentary law.[21] For the freshmen law students these clubs seem to have served somewhat the same purposes that the Debating Society had served at an earlier period, to train them in the art of expression and in impromptu speaking and discussion. Announcement of the "Eleven" Clubs continued only until the end of the Konop era, 1941–1942.

At the opposite end of the spectrum from the clubs for the freshman law students was a Bureau of Research in Educational and Civil Church Law established toward the end of Dean Konop's tenure. This bureau had five objectives: 1) to supply to all interested persons memoranda on particular legal problems in the field of Civil Church Law; 2) to survey the legal status of schools and churches in all the jurisdictions of the United States, to be published state by state; 3) to publish monographs on particular abstract propositions of law pertinent to schools and churches; 4) to prepare an annual Digest of all cases involving Civil Church Law; 5) to conduct courses in Civil Church Law. This bureau, an excellent undertaking, was directed by Professor James J. Kearney who joined the law faculty in 1938, but it unfortunately ended when he left Notre Dame in 1942. During its short existence, Kearney published "A Memorandum on the Liability Created by a Mortgage on Church Property which is Held by an Ecclesiastic as a Common Law Trustee," a treatise on "Public Aid for Private and Sectarian Schools," "A Digest of Church Law Decisions of 1939," and "A Digest of Church Law Decisions of 1940."[22]

The success of its graduates in passing the bar examinations in their several states on first appearance before bar examination boards is not a primary gauge of a law school's quality, but it is an important measure of such quality, and every school takes pride when its graduates are uniformly successful. For the early years of the

Hoynes era, Notre Dame received praise and congratulations on the excellent record her graduates were marking up in bar examinations. Over the years this record has been uniformly good. In 1921 a law graduate of that year was moved to telegraph Dean Vurpillat, "Reports are that Notre Dame scored perfect record in the October Bar [Illinois] . . . and I wish to thank the Law Faculty for their untiring efforts. I wonder how many of the boys know what the Doctrine of Hotchpotch [Hotchpot] is. Notre Dame has a record to be envied."[23] But what is a good record on the bar examinations? Here the experts disagree. A 1937 news release from the university's Office of Public Information noted that "seventy-five percent of the 1937 graduates from the Notre Dame College of Law were admitted to the bar in various states." Then the writer added: "Dean Konop stated that this is an exceedingly high average for a class. He said the average is about fifty percent."[24] Several years later Dean Clarence Manion in a letter to Father Howard Kenna, Vice-President for Academic Affairs, implies that eighty percent success of the current graduates in passing their bar examinations was nothing to be proud of. He wrote, "The record of Notre Dame law graduates in passing the bar examinations in the several States has been uniformly good down through the years, but there have been deviations. Thus of the graduates who took the bar examinations in 1948, 20% failed."[25] And very recently Dean Joseph O'Meara wrote: "Eighty-five and five tenths percent of the Class of '67 passed the bar examinations on the first try—not a showing to be proud of." Then he added,

"Except for the disastrous results in one state, however, the percentage passing on the first try would have been 98.1."[26]

In conclusion a generally favorable judgment can be passed on Thomas Konop's years as dean. When he took over the leadership of the school it was at a low point both in organization and morale, and he left it well rehabilitated.

NOTES

1. Cf. *University Bulletin* (1924–25), 151; Special *College of Law Bulletin* (1927–28), 9; and the *University of Notre Dame du Lac,* 1934, p. 3. Notre Dame Collection, University Memorial Library.
2. For biographical data, cf. *Who's Who in Law,* I (1937), 524; *The Faculty of the College of Law, University of Notre Dame,* 1930; *Alumnus,* October 1937, 9 and 26.
3. *South Bend News-Times,* March 17, 1937.
4. *Bulletin of the College of Law* (1948–49), 17 ff.
5. *University Bulletin* (1925–26), 167. This announcement was repeated in the *University Bulletins* for many years.
6. *Bulletin of the College of Law* (1923–24), 17–18.
7. *University Bulletin* (1929–30), 188–189.
8. *Ibid.* (1940–41), 339.
9. *Ibid.* (1930–31), 187–188.
10. Cf. Chapter III, note 10.
11. This statement is based on a letter from Clarence Manion to the author, which is treated in detail in Chapter 5.
12. The members, in addition to Dean Konop, were Clar-

ence Manion, Elton Richter, Homer Earl, William Rollison, William Cain and James Kearney. Aaron Huguenard (1928–31) was also full-time member during the first year of the decade.

13. *University Bulletin* (1931–32), 218.
14. *Ibid.* (1930–31), 187.
15. *Bulletin of the College of Law* (1949–50), 8–9.
16. *University Bulletin* (1928–29), 198.
17. *Ibid.* (1942–43), 335.
18. *Bulletin of the College of Law* (1950–51), 9.
19. Membership in the American Law Student Association was first announced in 1950–51 when the name Law Club was changed to Student Law Association.
20. *Bulletin of the Law School* (1969–70), 18.
21. Cf. *University Bulletin* (1928–29), 198.
22. *Alumnus* (March, 1941), 13. Oddly, no mention of this Bureau is found in the official *Bulletins* of 1939–1942. The two Digests were published in the *Notre Dame Lawyer,* XV (1940), 307 ff. and XVI (1941), 318 ff. respectively. "Public Aid for Private and Sectarian Schools" appeared in *Yearbook of School Law* VIII (1940), 144 ff. *A Memorandum* was published in pamphlet form.
23. Henry W. Fritz to Vurpillat, October 11, 1921. UNDA, Vurpillat Papers.
24. News release, December 1, 1937. Office of Public Information, Konop file.
25. Manion to Kenna, March 2, 1948. Office of Vice-President for Academic Affairs, Manion file.
26. *Notre Dame Law School: Report of the Dean* (1967–68), 22.

5

The Manion Era 1941-1952

ON THE RESIGNATION OF THOMAS KONOP FROM THE OFFICE of dean in the spring of 1941, Clarence E. Manion, a professor in the law school, was appointed his successor. In a recent letter to the writer Mr. Manion wrote, "Thus undoubtedly, I am the only remaining official link between the beginning and the end of the Law School's first One Hundred years."[1] His claim to this distinction is firmly founded. He knew well the first dean of law at Notre Dame, William Hoynes, and William B. Lawless, who takes up the duties of dean in this centennial year, received his law degree from

Notre Dame during the Manion era. Mr. Manion first met Hoynes in September 1919, when he enrolled as a first-year law student, and after years of close association he was appointed administrator of the Hoynes estate in 1933. As student, professor and dean, he was associated with the law school for thirty-three years.

Clarence Manion was born in Henderson, Kentucky, in 1896. He attended St. Mary's College, Kentucky (a school that Father Sorin showed some interest in during the 1840s) from which he received his degree of bachelor of arts in 1915. Upon graduation, he won a Knights of Columbus graduate fellowship for the Catholic University of America, where he spent the next two years, earning the degree of master of arts in 1916 and the degree of master of philosophy in 1917. In 1919, as has been mentioned, he enrolled in law at Notre Dame. At the same time, he was appointed a part-time instructor of history. In 1922 he was one of the first students to receive from the university the degree of doctor of jurisprudence instead of the bachelor of laws. After completing his law studies, Manion practiced law in Evansville, Indiana, for two years, and was then invited to join the Notre Dame law faculty in 1924. While continuing his teaching duties, he served as Director of the National Emergency of the State of Indiana from 1935 to 1938. In 1941 he received appointment as dean. Since his resignation from this position eleven years later, he has been a member of the law office of Doran, Manion, Boynton and Kamm in South Bend.[2]

When Dean Manion resigned his position, it was immediately bruited across the country that he had been "fired" by the university, the alleged reason being his conservative politics. This was not true, and it would be a serious reflection on Notre Dame as a university if it were. The fact was that by 1952, Dean Manion had become so engaged in activities outside Notre Dame that he could no longer do justice to his duties as dean. Both he and the president of the university, Father John J. Cavanaugh, recognized this; Dean Manion submitted his resignation and Father Cavanaugh accepted it. To put an end to the rumor, Father Cavanaugh made a public announcement which was widely distributed, in which he quoted excerpts from the dean's letter of resignation. In his announcement Cavanaugh said that Dean Manion had resigned because "the pressure of private business, together with a constantly lengthening schedule of writing and speaking commitments, now makes it physically impossible for him to continue to administer the affairs of the Law School." This was but a quotation from the dean's letter. Then the president went on to say, "Dean Manion, in his twenty-eight years on our faculty, and even in his undergraduate years in our College of Law, exemplified the qualities Notre Dame exists to implant. He has contributed in a singular way to American life. His career has marked the personal, the professional and the spiritual that add up to a remarkable epitome of what Notre Dame means by moral, responsible leadership."[3]

When Dean Manion took over the leadership of law at Notre Dame in the summer of 1941, he found it in a stronger position than it had been when any of his three predecessors assumed the duties of dean. But Pearl Harbor and World War II were less than six months ahead, and these events were to create a problem both harrowing and prolonged, that of a diminishing student body. The depression years of the 1930s had reduced the number of students from what it had been at the end of the 1920s, but the situation became critical only with the World War. Mr. Manion has described how precarious the very existence of the law school became, and in view of this description, it may be surmised that Dean Hoynes was faced with the same kind of situation when World War I broke out in 1917; it was probably this situation which in large part caused the conditions of which Francis Vurpillat complained in his letters to Fathers John W. Cavanaugh and James A. Burns.[4] Vurpillat said nothing explicitly about the number of students but he did emphasize the inadequate teaching staff; in the same vein Dean Manion was able to add no full-time faculty member to his staff between 1941 and 1946, while at the end of his first year he lost two full-time members.

The years of World War II were a trying period in the history of law at Notre Dame, albeit a challenging time as Mr. Manion now recalls it:

> My administration soon became known as the "famine and feast" period. The military draft was cutting into our enrollment when I took over and Pearl Harbor practically cleaned us out of all but the "4Fs." When the Abbé Seyes was asked what he did during the French Revolution, he replied, "I survived." This is my reply to the question of what the Law School did during the War Years. More than half of the

> American law schools closed down at least for some period during the War. Father Hugh O'Donnell [thirteenth president of the university] thought we should suspend and I talked him out of it only with the firm promise that I would cut down our expenses to the level of our tuition income. Literally, we were unable to do that, of course, but I came close to the mark by charging the Navy and the other Colleges of the University "room rent" for the use of our Law Building classrooms. . . . The one dubious "distinction" from which I sweated to escape was that of being the dean who closed "the oldest Catholic Law School in this country."

Besides the ploy of charging room rent to other units of the university, Dean Manion made great efforts to recruit students, presumably "4Fs," by writing and lecturing on the advantages of legal education at Notre Dame before bar associations and college audiences across the country. A fringe benefit of this activity was his receiving from Boston University an honorary degree of Juris Utriusque Doctoris. This so pleased Father O'Donnell that he authorized the dean to say that the Notre Dame Law School would remain open "for the duration." "Nobody," concludes the former dean, "but Father O'Donnell and I know how precariously we were walking the razor's edge of continuity. But we made it."[5]

With the ending of the war, the "feast" years of the Manion era in regard to student enrollment began. The student body jumped from around fifty to two hundred and twenty-five in two years, reached an all-time high of over three hundred in the late 1940s and then dropped back to around two hundred by 1952.

It was noted above that Dean Manion was able to add no full-time faculty member to the law staff between 1941 and 1946. During these years the only new member was Mrs. Lora Lashbrook who from 1942 to 1947 served as librarian, teacher of research, registrar, and secretary to both the dean and the faculty, and to whom Mr. Manion gives great credit for the survival of the law school during the critical war years. From 1946 to 1952, however, eleven full-time members joined the law faculty, five of whom remained for two years or less. In the spring of 1948, the Vice-President for Academic Affairs, Father Howard Kenna, wrote the dean: "I feel that the College of Law has made fine progress this year and I hope that it can be continued. I feel that the faculty members that you have recommended will be the equal of the young men we engaged last year and I am sure that the results will justify your judgment in the matter."[6] But something must have gone wrong because in the fall of 1948 a Mr. Jack Miller was the only new faculty member and he stayed only one year.

During the last six years of the Manion era nine part-time faculty members or lecturers also joined the staff. In the faculty lists given in the Appendix, attempt is made to distinguish them from full-time faculty members because today the term *lecturer* has supplanted the term *part-time faculty member,* at least at Notre Dame. In consequence it is necessary to distinguish between two categories of lecturers, those who hold faculty status and teach or lecture in the classroom and those who are invited in for a lecture or two at various times. The first category may be designated *regular lecturers,* the second, *special lecturers.* The regular lecturers are appointed to teach or lecture on a subject in substantive law or to conduct a course in practical law for which they are particularly qualified through specialization or through experience; the special lecturers are engaged to give the students opportunity to meet outstanding jurists and to broaden their perspective of the legal profession.

Recognition and tribute are due to all those members of the faculty who have given years of dedicated service to the law school, but the list of such men is too long to make acknowledgment of every individual feasible. However, in Chapter 2 Timothy E. Howard was singled out for recognition, and now like recognition can be made of a present member of the law faculty, Professor John J. Broderick. Professor Broderick came to Notre Dame in 1947. In 1932 he received the bachelor of arts degree *summa cum laude* from Washington and Lee University, and in 1936 the bachelor of laws from St. John's University Law School. Immediately upon leaving law school, he entered the graduate school of Public Administration at New York University as a graduate fellow. Then followed several years of practice, broken by a three-year stint in the Navy during World War II. Several years after he began his teaching career, Professor Broderick returned to New York University and completed work for the M.P.A. He has held the position of assistant dean of the law school for most of his twenty-two years at the university. Several generations of law students hold him in admiration and affection for his wise counselling, effective teaching, and devoted service as assistant dean. Expert in the field of labor law, he has for years represented the law school in the Labor-Management Conferences held each year at the university under the direction of the Reverend Mark Fitzgerald of the Department of Economics. A Phi Beta Kappa in his undergraduate years, Professor Broderick was in no small measure responsible for the Epsilon of Indiana Chapter of Phi Beta Kappa, installed at Notre Dame in February of 1968. For his long years of devotion to the university and dedicated service to the law school Notre Dame reveres his name.

The war was the occasion for a significant addition to the requirement for admission to the law school. As early as 1942–1943 the *University Bulletin* carried the notice: "As part of the accelerated program of the University for the wartime, the University Council has modified the minimum requirement for admission to the College of Law so that the student who has as much as sixty semester hours of acceptable credits for college work as preparation may be admitted to the three year course of law for the degree of bachelor of laws."[7] This announcement continued to appear until well into the 1950s, although in 1953 the minimum was raised to ninety semester hours or three years of college work. Then, as was remarked in the preceding chapter, in 1946 graduation from an approved college became mandatory admission requirement for all non-veterans except Notre Dame students who were in one of the combination programs.[8]

No change was made in the methods of instruction in the Manion era. The case method continued to be primary, supplemented by textbook assignments and lectures. In fact there was no noticeable change in teaching methods from 1905 until 1952. The aim of the law course also remained the same—to give students a thorough preparation for the practice of law in any State.

Small changes in the program of courses continued to be made, but substantially the curriculum remained stable. An example is the course program for 1946–1947, the half-way mark of the Manion era, and the last program for which Dean Manion was responsible, 1952–1953. The 1946–1947 Program: First Year: year course in Procedure I and II; semester courses in Contracts (5 hrs.), Torts (5 hrs.), Personal Property, Fundamental Law, Criminal Law, Bibliography (1 hr.), Domestic Relations, Landlord and Tenant, and Air Law; Second Year: year courses in Real Property I and II, Practice Court and Briefing I and II; semester courses in Evidence and Equity; Third Year: Practice Court and Briefing (1 hr. each semester), Private Corporations, Public Corporations, Constitutional Law and Conflict of Laws. The 1952–1953 program: First Year: year course in Procedure I and II; semester courses in Contracts (5 hrs.), Torts (5 hrs.), Criminal Law, Fundamental Law, Personal Property, Bibliography (1 hr.); Second Year: year course in Real Property I and II; semester courses in Bills and Notes, Legal Ethics, and Constitutional Law; Third Year: year course in Practice Court and Briefing (1 hr. each semester); semester courses in Constitutional Law, Legal Research, and

Mortgages. By 1952–1953 forty-six hours of electives were not only allowed but required to fill out the student's program, but in 1953–1954, under a new dean, electives were abolished.[9] In regard to electives, Dean Manion recommended to Father Kenna in 1948 that, besides Jurisprudence which was already offered, Roman Law, International Law and the History of English and American Law should be made available to the students as electives, the courses to be taught by qualified faculty members in other departments of the university.[10] In his reply Father Kenna approved this recommendation and suggested that they be made required courses,[11] but nothing came of this suggestion.

In view of the precarious situation in the law school during the war years, with its very survival in question, it is no surprise that there was little or no increase in library holdings during those years. After the war conditions improved and some six thousand volumes had been added by 1952, bringing the total holdings from approximately sixteen thousand volumes in 1941 to twenty-two thousand in 1952. Nevertheless, the building up of the library was still painfully slow. In 1945 Miss Marie K. Lawrence was appointed law librarian and she gave excellent service over the next twenty-one years.

The moot court did not change in its essential function in the preparation of the students for the law—to give them experience in practical law, improve their speaking skill, and sharpen their ability to think on their feet in the midst of argumentation—but it was brought into greater prominence and made more meaningful in 1950, when Moot Court Competition was adopted at Notre Dame. This competition was a growing activity among American law schools and included three phases, local, regional and national competitions. The first announcement of this competition read: "The Notre Dame Moot Court Competition was inaugurated in the second semester of 1950 as an activity of the Student Law Association. . . . It is on a voluntary basis, used as a device of Appellate Procedure, and is open to all students in the law school."[12] Eligibility to enter the competition was later restricted; first-year students were required to brief and argue at least one appellate case each semester, but the competition was open to second-year students. The four men who survived the elimination rounds in that year were paired into two teams, representing plaintiff and defendant, in a final argument held in the fall of their third year before the University Court, which later would be dubbed the Supreme Court of the State of Hoynes, in memory of the first dean of law at Notre Dame. The four students prepared briefs and presented arguments and rebuttals before a panel of three judges. The judges scored the four on the basis of briefs submitted and arguments and rebuttals presented; the two highest were announced the winners. Until 1961 when Notre Dame became dissatisfied and dropped out of the regional and national competitions, the winning students became a team to represent the law school in these competitions, and did so with fair success. In 1950, the first year in competition, Notre Dame won the regional competition and went on to represent the Seventh Circuit Court of

DEANS OF THE NOTRE DAME LAW SCHOOL

William Hoynes
1883–1919

FROM
1883
TO
1968

Francis Vurpillat
1919–1923

Clarence Manion
1941–1952

Joseph O'Meara
1952–1968

Above:
Thomas Konop
1923–1941

Appeals of Chicago in the national competition, held in New York. The regional was also won in 1951, 1956 and 1957.

The adoption of the moot court competition was one of the achievements of the Manion era. To show his continuing interest in the competition, the Clarence E. Manion Award is still annually conferred on the winning students—their names are added to a plaque which hangs in the law library. In addition, cash awards were at first made by the Notre Dame Law Association; for several years now the cash awards have been contributed by A. Harold Weber, a prominent alumnus and member of the Law Advisory Council of the university.

Two activities in practical law were introduced in the last years of the Manion era, a Practicing Law Institute and Court Attendance. The first was held for the first time in 1949 as a Federal Tax Institute, but quickly broadened its scope. It was a two-day meeting, divided into several sessions. The *Bulletin* announcement reads simply: "Once a year Practice Law Institutes are held at the Law School under its auspices, in cooperation with the Indiana Bar Association. Members of the law faculty and prominent attorneys conduct the sessions."[13] The second was inaugurated in 1949: "Each student in the Law School is required to attend sessions of the local Federal and/or Circuit and Superior Courts for at least ten hours a semester."[14] These activities were dropped after 1952.

Two other important achievements during the Manion era were the establishing of a Natural Law Institute and the founding of the Notre Dame Law Association by the law alumni. In its teaching of the positive substantive law and in developing the skills which a lawyer must have in the practice of his profession, the Notre Dame Law School does not differ from other American law schools. But as the law school of a Catholic university, it has from its beginning aimed to integrate the teaching of positive law with a natural law philosophy or to ground its teaching of the positive law in a natural law philosophy. With the passing years this aim became more explicit and emphasis on a natural law philosophy has been achieved in several ways. One of these ways has been through the *Notre Dame Lawyer,* as noted in an *Alumnus* article, "Progress of the College of Law": "The College of Law was one of the first to place in its curriculum a special course in jurisprudence having for its purpose the direct integration of law and philosophy. The *Notre Dame Lawyer* . . . is devoting much space to the development and dissemination of a scholastic philosophy of law. Many articles have been published on Natural Law and its relations to other philosophies, so that it truthfully may be said that the *Notre Dame Lawyer* has become the organ of Scholastic jurisprudence among the periodicals of the legal profession."[15]

The inauguration of the Natural Law Institute was a second and even more explicit means of emphasizing a natural law philosophy as foundation for the teaching of positive law. The first Institute was held in the law building December 12 and 13, 1947. In his letter to the writer, former Dean Manion wrote: ". . . its establishment grew out of the Great Books seminars that we began in 1945 with the help of Judge Roger Kiley of Chicago and Father John Cavanaugh,"[16] then vice-president of the university. These seminars were monthly discussions of Judge Kiley of the Appellate Court of Illinois and Father John Cavanaugh with a selected group of law students on the nature of justice, based on comparative readings from Plato, Aristotle, St. Thomas Aquinas, Locke, Blackstone, Montesquieu and others.[17]

The function of the Natural Law Institute, as conceived by those who inaugurated it, is best stated in the *Bulletin* for 1951–1952, several years after the first Institute convocation was held: "The Natural Law has been an integral part of the training of a Notre Dame lawyer since the first law courses were established in 1869. The College of Law thus carries on the basic Natural Law philosophy of the American Founding Fathers and seeks not merely to set forth the abstract concepts of the Natural Law but also to correlate them with the various courses of the Positive Law. . . . In 1947 the College of Law founded the Natural Law Institute to extend this approach to legal study beyond the narrower limits of formal classroom instruction."[18] The purpose of the Institute is well expressed in a pamphlet *Notre Dame's College of Law* (pp. 14–15), published in 1952: "It is the purpose of this Institute to re-examine and re-state the doctrine of the Natural Law in the light of modern times and changing situations. To the annual sessions of the Institute . . . are invited the foremost lawyers, judges, legal philosophers and scholars at home and abroad to lead the discussions participated in by all who wish to attend."

During the five years that the Institute held its annual meetings, prominent jurists, legal philosophers and scholars from both "at home and abroad" appeared on the program. Those who founded the Institute had a well-defined position on the meaning of natural law and on its fundamental importance in determining or assessing the validity of all positive law. This position finds its more remote roots in Greek and Scholastic philosophy, and its proximate foundation in the writings of such great English jurists as Sir Edward Coke (1552–1634) and Sir William Blackstone (1723–1780), who championed a necessary relation between the natural law and the common law of England, and whose legal teachings profoundly influenced Jefferson and the other authors of the Declaration of Independence and of the American Constitution. Nevertheless, the Institute did not identify itself with any particular position, school or doctrine of natural law, as is evident from the papers read at the convocations, but was open to the investigation and discussion of various conceptions of the meaning of natural law and its role in the formulation of positive law and in the solution of concrete problems.

The papers read at the annual meetings of the Institute were published as *Natural Law Institute Proceedings,* and the resulting five monographs are a valuable contribution to the perenially important subject with which they deal. For his sponsoring of these publications and for his initiating the Natural Law Library at Notre Dame, the university is indebted to Alvin A. Gould. Mr. Gould's generosity was acknowledged in this official announcement: "At the Third Convocation of the Natural Law Institute held December 9 and 10, 1949, there was inaugurated in the College of Law the Natural Law Library. The initial collection of books was given to the Natural Law Library by Alvin A. Gould, the sponsor of the Second and Third Natural Law Institutes. It is the purpose of the library to collect and to make available for research all existing materials which will be of value in studying the natural law and in promoting its application."[19]

The Notre Dame Law Association was founded at an organizational meeting convoked on June 5, 1948 in the Law Building. It had, however, been in the making since September 1946, when a few law alumni were called together at the South Bend home of Francis Jones, who was to become the association's first president, and a planning committee appointed. The official announcement of the association sets forth its purpose and also some of its projected activities: "The Notre Dame Law Association, an organization of Notre Dame men in the legal profession, was organized in the June of 1948. In addition to fostering loyalty among the members . . . , its purpose is to inject a moral responsibility into the practice of law through the introduction of the Natural Law philosophy of jurisprudence. Initial objectives are the publication of a Legal Directory, procuration of qualified students, and counselling and placement service for those Notre Dame graduates interested."[20] In the minds of those participating in its founding the association was to serve the law alumni directly and the law school only indirectly. Some stress was also put on its independence of the university. The association was to be composed of law alumni, to serve their interests and to be managed and controlled by them. This independence has been maintained but with the passing years it has also been of great, direct help to the law school.

At the organizational meeting, attended by ninety-three alumni, a constitution and bylaws were adopted. In these the governance of the association was invested in the officers and a board of directors. The officers were honorary president, president, vice-president, secretary-treasurer, and executive secretary; the board of directors was composed of fifteen members. The first officers were Clarence Manion, Honorary President, Francis Jones, President, Charles Vaughn, Vice-President, Hugh Wall, Jr., Secretary-Treasurer and Robert E. Sullivan, Executive Secretary. The president of the association was also the president or chairman of the board of directors. An executive committee made up of officers and members of the board was appointed. Later the office of secretary-treasurer was separated into two offices; the board increased in numbers as time went by, and today has forty-two members.

An item in the minutes of the preliminary meeting held in 1946 reads: "Publication: *The Notre Dame Lawyer,* supplemented by a News-Letter." Although the *Lawyer* has been sent to all members from the outset, it in no sense ever became a publication of the association. As for the News-Letter, a resolution was passed in a meeting on June 9, 1951: "Resolved: that the Notre Dame Law Association, in view of the necessity of keeping its members informed of the affairs of the Association and to accomplish the objectives of advancing the cause of legal education and of injecting a moral responsibility, into the legal profession through the leadership of Notre Dame men, authorizes and approves the publication and distribution quarterly of the official organ of the Association, entitled *The Law Association News*." But this publication lapsed within a year and has never been re-instated. However, members are kept abreast of the activities of the association through various mailings from the central office.

The Notre Dame Law Association was just getting well underway when the Manion era ended. The minutes of the association's early meetings illustrate the dedication of its founders and early officers, but also show a basic defect not in organization but in operation. For years the executive secretary was either a faculty member or a local attorney, for whom management of the association or promotion of its activities were merely adjunct to their pressing academic or professional duties. In spite of much good will, the affairs of the association necessarily suffered. Dues-paying members, for example, numbered 230 in the first year and rose to 530 two years later, but there the number leveled off for several years. Also a *Legal Directory* was published, but efforts to keep it current were without much success, and other activities lagged. Nevertheless, the great potential of the association was always recognized and there have always been law alumni who have given unselfishly of their time and effort to fulfill this potential. The process of fulfillment continues to the present day, as shall be seen in Chapter 6.

NOTES

1. Manion to Moore, January 30, 1969.
2. *Who's Who in America* (1968–69), 1400.
3. *Alumnus* (January-February 1952), 7.
4. Cf. Chapter III, notes 1 and 3.
5. Manion to Moore, January 30, 1969.
6. Kenna to Manion, March 17, 1948, Office of the Vice-President for Academic Affairs, Manion file. Of the young men brought in in 1947, Edward Barrett and John Broderick are presently on the law faculty. Other present members who joined the faculty during the Manion era are Thomas Broden, Anton Hermann Chroust and Roger Peters.
7. *University Bulletin* (1942–43), 334.
8. Manion to Moore, January 30, 1969. Former Dean Manion calls attention to one exception for students in other schools. Arrangement was made with DePauw University and Wabash College to admit their students to freshman law on completion of three years of college work. Then these schools conferred their bachelor degrees on such students at the end of one year of successful study at Notre Dame.
9. For the programs of courses in 1946–47 and 1952–53, cf. respectively *Bulletin of the College of Law* (1946–47), 9–10, and (1952–53), 11–12.
10. Manion to Kenna, January 30, 1948, Office of the Vice-President of Academic Affairs, Manion file.
11. Kenna to Manion, February 24, 1948, Office of the Vice-President of Academic Affairs, Manion file.
12. *Bulletin of the College of Law* (1950–51), 9–10.
13. *Ibid.* (1950–51), 19.
14. *Ibid.* (1949–50), 9.
15. *Alumnus* (March 1941), 13.
16. Manion to Moore, January 30, 1969.

17. *Bulletin of the College of Law* (1949–50), 18. Later Great Books seminars were made obligatory for all first- and second-year law students and were conducted by the students themselves under the direction of faculty members. For senior students seminars were optional but most of them attended the discussions led by Judge Kiley and Father Cavanaugh to the end of the Manion era. Cf. *Notre Dame's College of Law* (1952), 12.
18. *Ibid.* (1951–52), 18.
19. *Ibid.* (1951–52), 7–8.
20. *Ibid.* (1949–50), 9.

6

The O'Meara Era 1952-1968

ON THE RESIGNATION OF DEAN MANION, A SYSTEMATIC search was begun to find a successor. A list of some twenty names was compiled, most of them members of the law schools of the country, and each man on the list was evaluated according to his legal education, academic and practical experience, publications, recognition received from the legal profession, and so on. Before this lengthy process was completed and a dean appointed, an alumnus of the university sent the president, Father John J. Cavanaugh, a letter written by Mr. Justice Wiley Rutledge in recommendation of a Mr.

Joseph O'Meara, practicing lawyer in Cincinnati, and advised him that Notre Dame would do well to interview Mr. O'Meara. Father Cavanaugh acted on this advice, invited Mr. O'Meara to the campus, and called together the interviewing committee. There was a great deal of skepticism among the members of this committee; the name O'Meara was not on the list of men under consideration and no one had ever heard of Joseph O'Meara. But this skepticism dissipated as the searching interview proceeded, and after the interview, the decision was reached to offer Mr. O'Meara the appointment, a decision which has never been regretted.

Joseph O'Meara was born in Cincinnati on November 8, 1898. He received the bachelor of arts degree from Xavier University and the bachelor of laws degree from the University of Cincinnati's College of Law. Admitted to the Ohio bar in 1921, he continued in the practice of law in Cincinnati and in Columbus until his appointment as dean, bringing to that office the rich experience of thirty-one years. Both before and after his coming to Notre Dame he was honored by a large number of appointments to committees and commissions, but more important, perhaps, were the appointments he turned down after becoming dean. For example, in 1956 Mr. John P. Frank, former professor of law at Yale University, wrote the dean that he would like to present his name to the President of the United States for appointment to the Supreme Court as replacement of Mr. Justice Sherman Minton.[1] In his refusal to have his name recommended for this high office, Dean O'Meara wrote, "I came to Notre Dame to do a job and, God willing, I mean to stay and finish it."[2] A job, of course, is never finished, but when he retired twelve years later, he left behind him the strongest small law school in the country. One indication of this was given by the Ohio bar several years before Dean O'Meara's retirement. In a survey covering the results of students from out-of-state schools taking the Ohio bar examinations over an eleven year period the statement occurs:

> Messrs. Diefenbach and Glenn selected the four law schools—Harvard, Michigan, Notre Dame and Yale—because the four out-of-state schools . . . are, or at least include, the best in the country. Furthermore, these four schools have more bar examination takers than other out-of-state law schools and therefore form the basis for a reliable statistical sample.[3]

To be ranked with Harvard, Michigan and Yale is encomium of which any law school can be justly proud.

In a meeting of the faculty early in his first year Dean O'Meara stated in regard to the admission of students to the law school: "There are two schools of thought. One, the so-called Harvard approach, tends to admit all with degrees and fail those who reveal inadequacies. The other view, the so-called Yale approach, favors selectivity in admissions and anticipates few failures. I favor the Harvard approach."[4] At the outset, therefore, Dean O'Meara favored admitting to the law school all students who held a bachelor's degree from an approved college or university. He also thought that all Notre Dame students who were in good standing should be admitted to the combination programs. But experience quickly changed his thinking. After a couple of years, all applicants were required to take the Law School Admission Test, prepared and administered by Educational Testing Service, Princeton, New Jersey. With each passing year admission standards were raised and selectivity increased. This was reflected in the attrition rate of students admitted; in Dean O'Meara's first years attrition ran as high as 40 percent for first-year students and to relatively high percentages for those in the second and third years; in the last year of the era, attrition was down to 2.4 percent for first-year men and to zero for second- and third-year men. Ever greater selectivity resulted from two other factors, the determination of the dean that the Notre Dame Law School remain small, never to exceed 300 students, and the increase in applications for admission which rose from 126 in 1954 to 502 in 1967. One other change in the admission requirements must be noted: beginning with the school year 1953–1954, war veterans were required to have completed three years of college instead of the two which had been the regulation for the preceding ten years.

The aim or purpose of legal instruction at Notre Dame remained substantially the same in the O'Meara era as it had always been, to produce the lawyer well grounded in the fundamentals of the law, trained in the essential skills of the practitioner, and deeply imbued with a sense of the moral responsibilities of the members of the legal profession. But this aim or purpose was more constantly insisted upon and expressed in several different ways. The fullest and best expression was achieved in the final *Bulletin* of the era:

> Drawing inspiration . . . from the Christian tradition, the Law School, while aiming first of all at technical proficiency, aims at more than that. Its primary purpose is to impart the knowledge and cultivate the skills a lawyer needs to represent his clients efficiently in a twentieth century workaday world. But professional competence is not enough. The Law School believes that lawyers and law schools must face the great questions concerning the nature of man and of society, the origin and purpose of law and the lawyer's role in society. These questions are given searching examination throughout the curriculum, particularly in a course on the Lawyer's Professional Responsibility in the first year, and a course in Jurisprudence in the second year. Thus the School systematically endeavors to illuminate the great jurisprudential issues which . . . insistently press for answer; and to make clear the ethical principles and inculcate the ideals which should actuate a lawyer. The School believes that the lawyer is best served, and the community as well, if he possesses not only legal knowledge and legal skills but also a profound sense of the ethics of his profession —and something else which the curriculum is likewise designed to cultivate: pride in the legal profession and a fierce partisanship for justice. To that end the Law School participates in a local program to provide legal services, mainly in civil cases, to persons unable to pay counsel. This activity is part of the Legal Services Program of the Office of Economic Opportunity.[5]

This statement not only sets forth in detail the objectives of the law school but also indicates in part how they are to be achieved—through the program of courses and legal aid to the poor. Another important means to their achievement has been the methods of instruction, which underwent significant changes during the O'Meara years.

In the early years of law at Notre Dame, law was taught through textbooks and class lectures, methods common to all law schools at the time. Then gradually the case method came into use and became the primary method by 1905. For almost fifty years this method was dominant in all three years of the law course, supplemented by textbooks and class lectures which were never abandoned, although today they are reduced to a minimal role. Since 1953 a rigorous case method has been retained in the first year but in the second and third years of the law program, it has been replaced by the problem method. The case method is intended to develop the power of diagnosis through intensive training in analysis, a skill essential to the lawyer. The problem method, in which the student learns the law by using it, is intended to develop ability "to find the law," to use the library efficiently. The problem method also develops the powers of interpretation, adaptation and creative utilization of the law; it trains the student in synthesis, the bringing together the law, seeing it as a whole so that it can be creatively utilized.[6] Case and problem methods, therefore, complement each other. A fringe benefit is that shifting to the problem method in the second year can prevent the boredom which the case method might bring on if used more than one year. Both methods recognize that the primary purpose of the classroom is not to impart complete information or knowledge, but rather to guide students in self-education by clarifying issues, correlating legal principles, stimulating interest and promoting understanding of the law. The problem method is especially conducive to this self-education. Perhaps it was for this reason that Mr. Howard C. Westwood, member of the Board of Visitors of Columbia University Law School, expressed the view, after visiting second and third year classes, that Notre Dame was doing a more constructive job of teaching the law than any other law school in the country.[7]

Diagnosis and analysis, synthesis and creative utilization of the law are at once abilities essential for achieving knowledge of the law and for developing skills indispensable to its successful practice. Other necessary practical skills, as every lawyer knows, are those of speaking easily and persuasively, marshalling arguments, thinking clearly under the stress of argumentation, and writing precisely and effectively. The first three of these skills are today, as always, developed principally in the law school courts, and to develop the students' writing skill a writing program was introduced in 1960. This program extended over the three years. In the first semester of the first year, in the Introduction to Law course, the student was given a thorough grounding in the use of the library. Emphasis was on research technique. At the beginning of the second semester, he was required to brief and argue an appellate moot court case; the emphasis shifted to writing technique. In the second year, the students were divided into groups of seminar size and each group was placed under the direction of a member of the faculty. Four research papers were assigned to each student and these were criticized and graded not only on the basis of their legal content but also on the basis of clarity and coherence. In the last year the program became less formal but more professional and emphasis was on briefs, memoranda of extensive research undertaken in one of the elective research seminars available to third-year students and on memoranda for use in court by counsel assigned to represent indigent prisoners.[8] In addition, of course, the students who earned places on the *Notre Dame Lawyer* and those who engaged in the moot court competition were afforded special opportunity to sharpen and refine their writing skill. Finally, a two semester-hour course in Legal Research and Writing was included in the prescribed program.

A radical change in the examination system was a second significant change in the instructional methods adopted from the beginning of the O'Meara era. Previously, examinations had continued to be given as Professor Vurpillat had described and complained of in 1918: at the end of each semester a completely separate and independent examination was given in each course by the individual teacher. These examinations in individual courses are still given but in addition comprehensive, cumulative examinations are held at the end of every semester, and the questions are so devised that the co-operation of the faculty working as a team is required in their preparation. In other words, at the end of each semester students are examined not only in the courses of the semester but also on all subject matter covered up to that point; at the end of the first year they are examined not only in the courses of the second semester but also on the courses of the entire year, and so on to the end of the sixth semester, when they are held responsible not only for the courses of that semester but for all subject matter of the three-year program. Moreover, questions in the comprehensive examinations are not labeled—e.g. Evidence, Contracts, Equity, Torts—but cut across several subjects, just as cases brought by clients to lawyers do. Such examinations oblige students to consistent study and continuous review. This results not only in the retention of their legal knowledge throughout their years of study but also in a gradual comprehension of the unity of the law and in a deeper understanding of the law. This constant review is also excellent preparation for bar examinations. To assure complete impartiality students remain anonymous and their examination papers, usually typed, bear only a number which they have drawn just before the examinations begin. Unproctored examinations—the so-called Honor System—were first proposed to the students in 1955 and put into effect for those students who voluntarily chose them. Since 1960 every law student has freely chosen the honor system and all examinations have been unproctored.

In the early years of law at Notre Dame, the program of courses was prescribed; there were no elective courses available to students, and this remained true down to the Konop era. This may have been a set policy or necessitated by the small faculty, but more probably it was simply a conformity to general procedure in most American law schools. Be that as it may,

Dean Thomas Konop introduced electives into the law curriculum, reasoning that since it was impossible to cover all aspects or areas of the law in a three-year program, each student should be permitted to build on a few prescribed fundamental courses his own full program of courses in accordance with his particular interests. Once introduced, the elective courses grew in number and by 1951–1952, as was pointed out in the preceding chapter, forty-six semester hours of a student's program were earned in electives.

With the advent of Dean O'Meara, the elective system was eliminated, although toward the end of this era a small choice was made available to third-year students. Ironically, the principal reason for eliminating electives was substantially the same reason that had been given for adopting them—since it was impossible to cover all aspects or areas of the law in a three-year program, a sound legal education should be limited to those courses which the faculty judged to be of most value in the preparation of lawyers. A supporting reason was that the elective system meant specialization, which Dean O'Meara held to be undesirable for students in a bachelor of laws program. And so a required program of courses was settled upon and put into effect in 1953–1954. It should be noted that the minutes of meetings of the faculty in 1952–1953 reveal that the subject of curriculum was heatedly debated throughout almost the entire year and some strong arguments were advanced in support of electives in the program. In the end, however, the vote to adopt the prescribed program was unanimous.

This program was as follows: First Year: year courses in the History of the Legal Profession, Contracts, Torts, and semester courses in Introduction to Law, Criminal Law, Legislation, Agency, Property I and Procedure I (Legal Writing and Research); Second Year: semester courses in Equity, Constitutional Law, Property II, Procedure II (Pleading and Practice), Procedure III (Evidence), Business Associations, Administrative Law, Labor Law, and a Natural Law Seminar, conducted throughout the year; Third Year: year courses in Jurisprudence, Federal Taxation, Estate Planning, and semester courses in Sales, Bills and Notes, Procedure IV (Practice Court), Fiduciary Administration, Credit Transactions, and Conflict of Laws.

This first program remained remarkably stable throughout the sixteen years under Dean O'Meara, but it also shows a flexibility which permitted it to meet changes in the legal situation, new areas of growing importance. A comparison of it with the last program of the era brings out the following differences: 1) Equity, the Natural Law Seminar, Sales, Bills and Notes, Estate Planning, and Fiduciary Administration have dropped out as designated courses, although their subject matter is treated in other courses; 2) Government Regulation of Business, Family Law, Secured Transactions and a Senior Seminar are new course titles; 3) History of the Legal Profession is replaced by Professional Responsibility; 4) Procedure courses have been increased from four to five with broader subject matter; and 5) there is some shifting in the order of courses in the program.

Except that Notre Dame dropped out of the regional

and national competitions in 1961, the moot court and the moot court competition remained in the O'Meara era pretty much the same as they were in the Manion era. But an innovated court was inaugurated in 1953—the Practice Court, which was a course in the prescribed program. Because of the importance placed on this practice court in the legal program, it seems well to cite its official description:

> Each student must try a complete jury case in the "Superior Court of the State of Hoynes," which follows, in the main, the Federal Rules of Civil Procedure and the Federal Rules of Criminal Procedure. Student counsel interview parties and witnesses, and prepare and file pleadings and trial briefs. Motions before trial and after verdict are heard in The Law School and a jury of first year students is impanelled on the afternoon preceding trial. All trials are conducted on Saturdays before U.S. Circuit Judge Luther M. Swygert, who serves as chief judge, and before judges of the United States District Court for Northern Indiana and the Superior Court of St. Joseph County in their respective courtrooms. Faculty members from the various colleges of the University, their wives, local business and professional men and women, and members of the South Bend Police Department serve as parties and witnesses. The aim of the Practice Court is to broaden the understanding and deepen the insight of the students—not only the upperclassmen who try the cases but also the first year men who serve as jurors—and to achieve this greater understanding and insight through active participation in the resolution of controversy by jury trial—the

> process which is central to and characteristic of our legal system.[9]

Full credit for the practice court goes to Professor Edward F. Barrett, its innovator. This is but one of the important contributions Professor Barrett has made to the law school since he joined its faculty in 1947 and for which he has the gratitude of all at Notre Dame who know of his work. Acknowledging these contributions, Dean O'Meara wrote several years ago, "His greatest achievement, in my opinion, is our Practice Court, which is almost solely his creation. It generates more intense interest than any other feature of our program of instruction, and far surpasses any other practice court anywhere."[10]

The methods of instruction, the curriculum and the courts accomplished in part the aims of legal education in the O'Meara era, the education of knowledgeable, proficient lawyers. The rest of the aim, the inculcating in the students a deep sense of moral responsibility, a pride in the legal profession and fierce partisanship for justice, has been carried out through specific courses in the program which have varied somewhat throughout the years. In the beginning they were History of the Legal Profession, a Natural Law Seminar and Jurisprudence for first-, second- and third-year students respectively. Later the Natural Law Seminar was combined with Jurisprudence and History of the Legal Profession was replaced by Professional Responsibility, which seems to be a more developed, improved course content of what was intended in the earlier course. Although this content extends far beyond the lives and writings of some of the great men of the legal profession, these are held up to the students as models, "whose principles and ideals, courage and devotion reflect the canon of professional ethics in which they were grounded."

In the Manion era the building up of faculty progressed and at its end there were eight full-time and four part-time members on the staff. The time was past when a professor could write that he was carrying a teaching load that in other prominent law schools would be distributed among three professors. Under Dean O'Meara the increase continued and by 1968 there were twelve full-time and nine part-time members on the faculty. Since student enrollment did not go up, this increased number made possible for the first time the granting of leaves of absence to faculty members, and one or two men were on leave every year from the mid-1950s to 1968. It also enabled men to participate more widely, both at home and abroad, in conferences, symposia and meetings, to serve on various legal committees, and to devote some time to consultantships. Finally, though in the past faculty members had produced a fair number of publications, the reduced teaching schedules during the O'Meara years resulted in a notable increase of books and articles in legal journals. One publication, which received international recognition and therefore may fittingly be singled out for mention, was the monumental study of the history of contraception from "genesis to genetics" as set forth in the writings of Catholic theologians and canonists, by Professor John T. Noonan, *Contraception: A History of its Treatment by the Catholic Theologians and Canon-*

ists.[11] Of his faculty, Dean O'Meara could also say, "I don't believe that any group of men could work together more devotedly, more cooperatively, more industriously than this Faculty has done."

Student enrollment was 222 in 1952. The next September it had jumped to 244, but then it gradually declined to a low of 150, in 1956 and 1957. Then began a steady climb, but it was almost ten years before the 1952 level was regained, 225 students in 1966. By September 1967 enrollment went to 258, and in September 1968 to 269. Several factors account for both the fall and rise of student enrollment, factors which can be distinguished but which must be considered together in judging their impact on enrollment. Enrollment dropped because of rising standards of admission, increased selectivity, the small number of applications, especially from Notre Dame students, for the combination programs without compensating applications from other schools for some years, heavy attrition of not only first-year students but also of second- and third-year students, and the high cost of legal education at Notre Dame coupled with lack of scholarships and other financial aid. The reasons for the steady rise of enrollment after the early years of the O'Meara era were correlative with the reasons for its fall, except for the first two, rising standards of admission and increased selectivity.

Rising standards of admission and greater selectivity strikingly reduced the number of first-year students during the years when applications were few, such as in 1954 when they numbered only 126. On the other hand, when the applications increased to 502 in 1966, this problem disappeared, although a limit on acceptances was maintained because of Dean O'Meara's determination to keep the Notre Dame Law School under 300 students.[12] Applications for combination programs began falling as early as 1953, and though they rallied for a while gradually decreased until 1969, when they numbered only six, and the combination programs have now been eliminated. The first drop in applications for the combination program seems to have been caused at least in part by a student grapevine; second- and third-year law students, reacting unfavorably to the higher standards and harder work, passed the word on to undergraduates not to apply for admission to law at Notre Dame. The later decline had two possible causes, a growing realization on the part of students that it would be better for them to complete college before going into law and the preference of the law school for applicants who held a bachelor's degree. This preference was not openly expressed, but it probably was inferred so that there was an interaction between these causes, the second having some influence on the first. At the same time, however, applications from students of other colleges and universities, Catholic and non-Catholic, private and public, grew steadily as a result of an intensive recruitment program and the widening reputation of the law school. The result of all this has been a tremendous change in the composition of the student body; in 1953, 82 percent were from the colleges of Notre Dame and 18 percent from other schools; in 1967, 77.5 percent were from other schools, and 22.5 percent were from Notre Dame; most of these had completed their college work. In 1968–1969, eighty-six colleges and universities are represented in the student body. Attrition rates have dropped from around 40 percent of first-year students and relatively high percentages of upperclassmen in the early 1950s to 2.4 percent of first-year students and zero percent of upperclassmen in the last year of the O'Meara era.

Before passing on to the final reason for the fall and rise of student enrollment during the years under consideration, it is appropriate to mention a significant change of policy which could conceivably modify the composition of the student body rather drastically in the years to come: in the school year 1965–1966 the first women students were admitted to the law school. "The old order changes, yielding place to new, and God reveals Himself in many ways."

The high cost of legal education at Notre Dame has perhaps always deterred students from applying for admission to the law school and also has caused a fairly large number of those applying to fail to register after they were informed of their admission. Tuition and fees have ranked with the most expensive law schools in private universities and have been more than double those in public or state universities, and this has become an increasingly acute problem. A generation ago parents were willing to finance the professional education of their children and the children were willing to accept this financial aid. Now a growing number of young men refuse to accept such aid even from parents who are able to give it. Also, costs have mounted not only absolutely but also relatively, with the depreciation of the purchasing value of money. To choose at random an illustration of this, in 1923 tuition and fees for a year of law at Notre Dame were $260 and the total cost for a year at the university was $847; in 1967 tuition and fees were $1,400 and the total cost was estimated to be $3,300. Competition among law schools for the most promising students has become as keen as that among college coaches for promising athletes. Other schools have been able to offer attractive scholarships not only to the best students but also to other applicants, whereas until 1952 the Notre Dame Law School had no scholarship funds, and the only financial assistance that could be offered prospective students was student employment, which was limited to a few. In the early O'Meara years these problems of costs were unquestionably one cause of the decline in applications for admission to law at Notre Dame and for the sharp drop in enrollment. An eventual growth in scholarship funds and other financial aids accounted in large measure for the steady increase in applications and enrollment in the later years of the era.

Aids other than scholarships have been loans and student employment. A student loan fund was established in 1959 in co-operation with the Continental Illinois National Bank and Trust Company of Chicago. Second- and third-year students could borrow five hundred dollars a semester up to a total of two thousand dollars for the four semesters. Loans were also available from the American Bar Association and from loan programs administered by the university's Office of Financial Aid. Student jobs requiring a service of twelve hours a week were allotted to a few law students who were judged able to carry the workload without injurious consequences to their legal education.

The growth of scholarship money since 1952, when there was not a dollar in the scholarship till, has been one of the more exciting episodes in the history of the law school. This growth has been almost entirely interwoven with development of the Notre Dame Law Association and a radical change in its purpose.[13] Chapter VI dealt with the founding of the association in 1948 and pointed out that its purpose was to promote a better community among its members, alumni of the law school, and to thereby further their interests. Only indirectly was it to benefit the university or the law school. One project devised to accomplish its purpose was the publishing of a current *Legal Directory* which would list the name and address of all Notre Dame lawyers by locality both in the United States and abroad. The weakness of the association, as was pointed out, was the lack of a central office with a paid full-time executive secretary who could efficiently do the work necessary to achieve the purposes, especially the publishing and constant up-dating of the *Legal Directory*. Nevertheless, the association continued to make progress, however haltingly, almost entirely because of the dedicated service of its officers and directors. But a contributing cause of this progress was a new direction, a new primary purpose for the association—the sponsorship of scholarship fund raising. Dean O'Meara lost little time in notifying the association of the urgent need of scholarship money, especially if Notre Dame were to compete for the best students, and he proposed that the association assume responsibility for the raising of money. The proposal was favorably received and in 1953–1954 a scholarship program was inaugurated, though it would be another four years before noticeable results appeared.[14] In 1957 the sum raised was just short of ten thousand dollars. The annual fund grew rapidly, but never quite rapidly enough to satisfy Dean O'Meara's expanding realization of what was necessary if Notre Dame was going to attract the quality of student that would make the law school great. When he first took his proposal to the association in 1953–1954, he said that twenty thousand in scholarship money must be made immediately available. Ten years later he stated ". . . we must have assurance for an absolute rock bottom minimum of $135,000 a year for scholarships."[15] This was quite a jump even for a ten-year span, and a larger jump to $275,000 was requested by Joseph O'Meara in his final year as dean.

Contributing to the steady growth of the annual scholarship fund were two developments, the establishment of name scholarships and the founding of the 500 Club. The name scholarships first appeared in 1955–1956 and numbered six in addition to the two in honor of Father John J. Cavanaugh; today they number sixteen; some are funded and some on annual basis. The 500 Club was founded in 1960, the inspiration of Mr. Albert H. Monacelli. As the name implies the goal of the club was five hundred members; the annual donation of each member was set at one hundred dollars. The halfway mark of membership was reached in 1967–68. While this club has given impetus to the growth of the scholarship fund, it could be a handicap in that older alumni financially able to give much more than a hundred dollars a year might limit themselves to the club donation.

In 1964 a very important event for the Notre Dame Law Association occurred—Mrs. Jeannette Allsop was hired as full-time executive secretary. Dean O'Meara reported several times that she was doing a superb job and officers and directors of the association who have worked with her are in hearty accord. Records and files in the central office were quickly put in order; by 1966 a completely revised edition of the *Legal Directory* was put out and an annual edition has appeared since; through the *Legal Directory* and regular communications out of the central office membership in the association increased from twenty-five hundred in 1964 to thirty-three hundred in 1969. The impact on the annual scholarship fund was not felt immediately but contributions rose from $86,000 in 1966 to $123,000 in 1967, and the amounts for 1968 and 1969 grew to $202,000 and $220,000 respectively. The amounts for corresponding years in the 1950s were $10,000 in 1957, $15,000 in 1958 and $21,000 in 1959.[16] Scholarships were awarded to 5 students in 1957 and to 98 in 1967; to 8 students in 1958 and to 143 in 1968; to 14 students in 1959 and to 152 in 1969. Cold statistics, these figures are nevertheless exciting. The Notre Dame Law School is now on a fairly competitive basis with the other strong law schools of the country, and its competitive position will probably improve steadily in the coming years.

When the law department was established in 1869,

its students had the same status as collegiate students in the university, and the thought of challenging this status most likely never occurred to anyone for many years. Possibly a question was raised around the turn of the century, for the status of the law students was officially spelled out for the first time in 1904–1905: "[Law students] are inmates of the University, authorized to attend the collegiate or other classes, subject to the rules of discipline prescribed for collegiate students, and entitled to equal rights and privileges."[17] They were also subject to the same academic regulations; law students at the time were of the same age and on the same educational level as all other collegiate students. Dean Francis Vurpillat seems to have been the first to complain about this and to underscore that law studies were professional studies and that law students should have a separate, professional status with appropriate disciplinary and academic regulations.[18] But no change of status was made, although as the years went by and completion of two, three and finally four years of college were required for admission to law, the students began to feel that they were above and apart from the general student body. If Deans Konop and Manion recommended a change, their efforts were ineffectual, and it remained for Dean O'Meara to take up where Dean Vurpillat left off some thirty years earlier, and to bring the issue to fruition. He insisted from the very outset that law students must be given a distinct status, a professional status which would engender a professional spirit or *esprit-de-corps* among them. In his first *Annual Report* he argued, and rightly, that in the Notre Dame context "college" denoted "undergraduate," and that the College of Law was simply one of the five colleges with undergraduate status. This militated against the fostering of a professional attitude and spirit; it lessened the prestige which law should have as a professional study; and it was not conducive to attracting to Notre Dame students from other colleges and universities who were required to have obtained the bachelor's degree before they were eligible for admission to law. As a first step toward extricating law students from undergraduate status, therefore, he fought for a change of name from College of Law to Law School; for him this change, small though it may seem in itself, was of great importance, and semantics were of genuine significance. Moreover, law school was the name generally used in American universities. Opposition to the change of name did not yield easily, but after two years the change was made in 1954–1955, and the new name appeared on the *Bulletin* for 1955–1956. Then step by step complete professional status was achieved. The final step, again small in itself, was the adoption in 1966 of an academic calendar distinct from the calendar for the rest of the university.

The growing inadequacy of the present law building, especially the library room, was mentioned in Chapter V. The situation grew gradually worse during Dean O'Meara's tenure. His repeated request for an addition to the building to meet the pressing needs went unanswered, but in the summer of 1964 modifications were made which buoyed the spirits of the dean temporarily: ". . . modifications have been made in the Law Building . . . which enable us to accommodate a student body of up to 275. . . . the Library is no longer a dungeon; for the first time since the building was erected, the Library is adequately lighted and comfortably furnished. Our seminar room has been enlarged; an additional office has been provided as well as space for two faculty secretaries. . . . These improvements . . . have transformed the building. It is still inadequate but I am hopeful that with our ingenuity we can solve what remains of the problem." He went on to say that stack space was still inadequate, then adds: "But space has been assigned for our exclusive use in the Memorial Library and little-used books will be transferred from time to time to this Law Library segment of the Memorial Library. . . . Not a desirable arrangement, but a viable one."[19] Under the stress of the inadequacies, however, this buoyancy soon disappeared.

In 1953 a special appropriation of fifty thousand dollars, to be expended over a five-year period, was made for the purchase of books, and by the end of the period library holdings had increased from approximately twenty-eight thousand to fifty-one thousand. By 1958, therefore, available stack space in the law library had been exceeded by approximately fifteen thousand volumes and in that year fifteen thousand volumes were put in dead-storage in the tower of the law building. Another important event of 1958 was the removal of the law library from the jurisdiction of the Director of University Libraries, as recommended by the Association of American Law Schools; it became autonomous under the dean and the law faculty. Under their direction was

Miss Marie Lawrence who became law librarian in 1945. Miss Lawrence had had years of library experience at the university before she transferred to the law library and of her the dean wrote: "She is described in a report on our Library, prepared by Professor A. C. Pulling, as 'one of the top librarians of the country.'" Professor Pulling, Director of the Harvard Law Library for many years, went on to say: "[Miss Lawrence] knows her bibliographies and what an excellent law collection should contain. As a result, she is building a well rounded out collection that will prove of inestimable value to faculty, students and those who may wish to carry on research. Miss Lawrence commands the respect of all law librarians, East and West."[20] Under her direction and that of her successors since 1966, Mr. and Mrs. Stanley L. Farmann, library holdings have been increased to approximately sixty-nine thousand volumes.

What are now called student activities have differed from era to era in the history of the law school from the founding of the Debating Society in the Hoynes era to the establishing of Gray's Inn in the O'Meara era. Those that survived two or more changes of administration, the Student Bar Association, the *Notre Dame Lawyer* and the Moot Court Competition, have been dealt with in earlier chapters. But here notes should be added to what has been said of the Student Bar Association and of the Moot Court Competition. In 1966, on recommendation of the executive board of the Student Bar, a Student-Faculty Coordinating Committee composed of three faculty members and three students was formed. The reason stated for the creation of this committee was "that the students and the Faculty have common concerns and that these concerns can best be pursued together rather than separately. The function and purpose of the Committee is to consider any problem or any issue that pertains to the Law School and to formulate policies which will enable the School to maintain and improve its academic standing."[21] In regard to the Moot Court Competition, during the Manion era the judges of the local competition were South Bend attorneys and State and Federal judges; throughout the O'Meara era a Justice of the Supreme Court of the United States acted as presiding judge, assisted by two Federal judges. The presence of a United States Supreme Court Justice greatly enhanced the prestige of the competition.

Gray's Inn was begun under Dean O'Meara as were a Legislative Bureau, a Legal Aid and Defender Association and a Law Wives Club. Gray's Inn, named for one of the four major Inns of Court, was founded in 1954 by the class that graduated in 1957, but for some reason it was announced for the first time in the *Bulletin* for 1960–1961. Its purpose is the discussion of current social, economic, scientific and cultural topics so that its members may be made more keenly aware of the social responsibility of the legal profession. These monthly discussions, held off campus in an informal atmosphere, are introduced by civic and business leaders, public officials and scholars who present an analysis of contemporary problems. The presentation is followed by general discussion during which the speakers may be subjected to vigorous questioning. The very existence of Gray's Inn witnesses to the alertness of the law students to the world they are living in as students and which they will face more immediately as lawyers.

The Student Legislative Bureau and the Legal Aid and Defender Association are service organizations. The bureau was established in the 1964–1965 school year. Its purpose is to "draft legislation at the request of legislators or others with substantial legislative programs. The actual drafting . . . is preceded by exhaustive research into existing law and legislation in other jurisdictions."[22] No small number, including several members of the Indiana General Assembly, have taken advantage of this service. Obviously, the exhaustive research into law and legislation is excellent training for the students.

The Legal Aid and Defender Association, established in 1965–1966, provides legal service to persons not able to pay legal fees. A year after its founding, it entered into a co-operative project to expand legal aid to the poor of South Bend. In conjunction with the St. Joseph County Bar Association, the St. Joseph County Legal Aid Society, the local Office of Economic Opportunity, the Community Action Agency and the local United Fund, a neighborhood law office was opened to which those who could not pay for private counsel could apply for legal help.[23] Motivated primarily by a desire to help the poor with their legal problems, the Legal Aid and Defender Association, like the Student Legislative Bureau, provides the students with excellent experiences for their future work as lawyers.

The Law Wives Club, or Barrister Wives, was formed

in 1955–1956, but announcement of it appears for the first time in a *Bulletin* for 1969–70. Its primary purpose is to foster the social and cultural life of law students' wives together with the wives of other Notre Dame students and of faculty members. But there is a secondary purpose—to give the women a better understanding of professional life and the life they will lead as wives of lawyers. A special event for the Barrister Wives each year is the sponsoring of a reception for the judges and lawyers attending the Final Argument in the Moot Court Competition.[24]

The Law Honors Banquet became more than a social event during the O'Meara era. Not only did it provide occasions to give recognition to students of outstanding achievement, but it also added to the prestige of the law school because the principal address at the annual dinner was delivered by the president of the American Bar Association.

The founding of the Natural Law Institute was one of the major achievements of the Manion era. Between 1947 and 1951 the Institute held five convocations at the law school in which prominent American and foreign jurists participated, and out of which came five published volumes of papers read at the convocations. On the advent of Dean O'Meara the convocations were discontinued but there was no intention of abolishing the Institute. On the contrary, in Dean O'Meara's first year discussions were begun on how the Institute could best accomplish its purpose. Scholars both at Notre Dame and from outside were consulted. Discussions and consultations were a search for a way in which the

Institute might function more effectively on a year-round rather than on a once-a-year basis. Late in 1953–1954 decision was reached to found a natural law journal which, it was hoped, could be published quarterly. This decision led to a meeting of seventeen distinguished men, representing various views on natural law, at the university on October 8 and 9, 1954. At this meeting the publishing of the journal, to be known as the *Natural Law Forum,* was definitely decided. This journal would comprise articles, notes or short communications, and book reviews. Its editor-in-chief would be assisted by a board of associate editors, and a large number of scholars around the world would be invited to serve as advisory editors. The first issue of the *Natural Law Forum* appeared in 1956, and the thirteenth issue, in 1969. Professor Antonio de Luna of the University of Madrid, who was a visiting professor at Notre Dame in 1956, was named the first editor-in-chief. The board of associate editors numbered ten, and the advisory editors, twenty-eight. On the return of Professor de Luna to Spain in 1957, Professor Anton-Hermann Chroust of the Notre Dame Law Faculty became editor-in-chief and served until 1961, when he was succeeded by Professor John T. Noonan, also of Notre Dame. In 1957 a managing editor was appointed, Professor Andrew Smithberger of the Notre Dame English faculty. The associate editors, men of outstanding scholarly distinction, were Vernon J. Bourke, St. Louis University; Anton-Hermann Chroust, Notre Dame Law School; George W. Constable, Baltimore; William J. Curran, Boston College Law School; H. P. d'Entrèves, Oxford

University; Lon L. Fuller, Harvard University Law School; Myres S. McDougal, Yale University Law School; F. C. S. Northrop, Yale University Law School; H. A. Rommen, Georgetown University; and Leo Strauss, University of Chicago.

An evaluation of the *Forum,* made shortly after the first issue appeared, is contained in a letter of Professor Filmer Northrop of the Yale University Law School and associate editor of the journal, to Dean O'Meara: "You and Professor de Luna and your Notre Dame colleagues must feel proud. The *Foreword* is superb, the *Statement of Policy* completely escapes the defensive for the positive and the concise, and the subsequent material sets a standard which must win the respect of scholars everywhere. . . . I deem it an honor to be asked to be an Associate Editor."[25]

The *Foreword* mentioned by Professor Northrop was written by Dean O'Meara; the *Statement of Policy,* a joint-announcement of the editors. Dean O'Meara wrote in part:

> How? is the job of the jurist, the legislator, the political scientist. And that job requires them endlessly to search out, assay and interpret facts, and to explore their interrelationships. But what facts are relevant? According to what standard are facts to be evaluated? What guide is to be used in seeking to interpret them? In these perplexities we regard natural law as a source of inspiration and guidance. . . .
>
> We are interested in exploring, with all the resources of scholarship and modern science, the full extent of the contribution natural law can make to the solution

> of today's problems. At the same time we do not expect detailed answers to specific questions. Too often "the natural law" has been dragooned by partisans to fight their wars. That is a danger we are very conscious of and mean to avoid. Illumination of problems—that is what we expect from natural law rather than a blueprint of detailed solutions.

The most significant paragraph in the *Statement of Policy* reads:

> The *Forum* will not be identified with any particular school or doctrine of natural law; nor will it rule out contributions which are basically opposed to the whole conception. We are interested in promoting a serious scholarly investigation of natural law in all its aspects, not in defending any established point of view. We will welcome any article in the area of philosophy, of social or behavioral science, or of jurisprudence, which leads to a more adequate understanding and evaluation of natural law, whatever its point of view may be; and we hope to publish relevant contributions from a maximum variety of sources. In this way it is our purpose to avoid the bias of any particular institutional orientation or political outlook, and thus to encourage the widest search for universal standards relevant to the solution of contemporary problems.

Thirteen years and thirteen issues after these words were written we can say that the *Natural Law Forum* has lived up fully to its expressed policy and that it has won in high degree "the respect of scholars everywhere" which Professor Northrop anticipated for it.

In concluding this account of the *Natural Law Forum,* some observations on it versus the convocations and published volumes of the Manion era must be made. Those who participated in the programs of the convocations were men of prominence but they did not measure up to the contributors to the *Forum* as legal scholars. The advantage of the convocations was the opportunity offered all who attended them to discuss at length the papers read and the views presented. But distinct advantages of the *Forum* seem to more than offset this advantage; in the convocations only the papers of those selected to appear on the programs made lasting contribution to the study of natural law; in the *Forum,* which is an established, internationally known journal, all scholars working in the area of natural law can submit writings for publication; this applies especially to the shorter writings published under Notes; and finally the book reviews in the *Forum* perform a valuable service to natural law students. One hope of those who founded the *Forum,* that it would quickly develop into a quarterly, has not been realized, and, therefore, it has failed in one objective—the functioning of the Natural Law Institute on a year-round rather than on a once-a-year basis.

From the day he took office, Dean O'Meara began planning a symposium on a subject of national interest. In his first year a Symposium on Legislative Investigations was held in the law school auditorium. These symposia became annual events in which lawyers, government officials and scholars in several fields participated.[26] They stimulated not only students and faculty members of the law school but also many others in both the university and the South Bend communities. An evaluation made by the writer in 1953 could be enlarged upon today: "... the Symposia and Conferences you are arranging to which are invited outstanding lawyers and men in government are giving new tone to the College and increasing its prestige."[27]

During the precarious years of World War II, the entire university was in many ways as much curtailed in its functioning as was the law school. This did, however, give time to think about and plan for the postwar years. One result of this planning was the inviting of some twenty prominent scientists, engineers and industrialists to serve on an Advisory Council for the Colleges of Science and of Engineering. This council met for the first time in October 1945. Notre Dame was not deceived in the help it anticipated from such a group of men in the areas of science and engineering, both on the undergraduate and graduate levels. When this first council was well established, the second council was set up in 1948—the Advisory Council for the College of Business Administration. Today there are advisory councils for the four colleges, the law school and other units of the university, such as the library. That an Advisory Council for the Law School be inaugurated was first proposed by Dean O'Meara in the *Dean's Report* for 1953–1954 and this proposal was acted upon in the following year. Presently there are twenty-one members of the council, and following the pattern of the other councils they have been chosen from both alumni and non-alumni and include non-Catholics as well as Catholics.

"Excellence is our platform and we can be content

with nothing less"—these words were repeated so many times by Dean O'Meara that they could well serve as legend on his academic coat-of-arms. They were a rallying call to all to whom they were addressed, students, alumni, faculty, university administrators, friends of the law school. To attain this excellence, wrote Dean O'Meara, "required, on the part of the Law School, the highest of standards and, on the part of the students, sustained hard work. In no other way can our graduates be properly prepared for the great responsibilities and opportunities that lie ahead." And on this rallying call the O'Meara era and the first century of law at Notre Dame ended. It has been said that excellence is relative, depending on time and circumstances, so that what is judged to be excellent at a given time may at later time be judged to fall considerably short of excellence. Perhaps it is better to say that excellence is never achieved but remains always a goal to be striven for, a goal which is never reached. But it can be said that at the end of the O'Meara era and the first century of law at Notre Dame, the law school reached the highest point on the curve of excellence that it had ever attained.

NOTES

1. Frank to O'Meara, September 21, 1956. Office of the Vice-President for Academic Affairs, O'Meara file.
2. O'Meara to Frank, September 27, 1956. *Ibid.*
3. 36 Ohio Bar 725 (July, 1963).
4. Minutes of Law Faculty Meeting, November 20, 1952.

5. *Bulletin of The Law School* (1968–69), 7.
6. Both research problem assignments and problems for immediate class discussion are used. Of these the research assignments are obviously more important; it is they that take the student to the library and lead him to learn the law by using it. Time allotted for out-of-class research problems varies from one to three weeks, depending on their complexity. Such a problem is assigned for every course in the second year, and in the third year one exhaustive research problem is given to each student for solution.
7. *Notre Dame Law School: Report of the Dean* (1958–59), 13.
8. Cf. *Bulletin of The Law School* (1968–69), 9–10.
9. *Ibid.,* 30–31.
10. *Notre Dame Law School: Report of the Dean* (1965–66), 23.
11. The author is keenly conscious that a list of publications by the law faculty during the century of law at Notre Dame would be valuable part of this history, but for several reasons attempt to compile such a list has not been undertaken.
12. Cf. *Notre Dame Law School: Report of the Dean* (1966–67), 7, where Dean O'Meara gives the reason for his insistence that the law school remain small: ". . . in a small school, more particularly our School, every teacher gets to know every student and every student gets to know every teacher and every other student. Thus we are a community come together to study law and committed to justice."
13. In 1954, Father Theodore Hesburgh, President of the University, established two law scholarships in honor of his predecessor, Father John J. Cavanaugh, but these are the only scholarships independent of the Notre Dame Law Association scholarship fund-raising efforts.

14. *Notre Dame Law School: Report of the Dean* (1955–56), 6.
15. *Ibid.* (1963–64), 5.
16. These figures are all rounded out numbers.
17. Special *Law Department Bulletin* (1904–05), 7.
18. Francis J. Vurpillat to John J. Cavanaugh, March 10, 1918. UNDA, Vurpillat Papers.
19. *Notre Dame Law School: The Dean's Report* (1964–65), 23–24,
20. *Ibid.* (1957–58), 16–17.
21. *Ibid.* (1966–67), 20.
22. *Ibid.* (1964–65), 12.
23. *Ibid.*, 11–12.
24. Cf. *Bulletin of the Law School* (1969–70), 18–19.
25. Northrop to O'Meara, September 1956. Office of Academic Vice-President, O'Meara file.
26. Among the subjects of these symposia in addition to Legislative Investigations were Role of the Supreme Court in American Constitutional System, Problems and Responsibilities of School Desegregation, Labor Union Power and the Public Interest, Next Steps to Extend the Rule of Law, Interstate Organized Crime, Violence in the Streets, Poverty and Justice, Fair Trial versus Free Press, the Challenge of Crime in a Free Society.
27. Moore to O'Meara, October 29, 1953. Office of the Vice-President for Academic Affairs, O'Meara file.

7

The Future

THE BEGINNING OF THE SECOND CENTURY OF LAW AT Notre Dame coincides with a new era, the deanship of William Burns Lawless, who assumed office in July 1968. A graduate in law from Notre Dame, a past president of the Notre Dame Law Association and former member of the Advisory Council for the law school, Dean Lawless also brings to his new position a rich experience of private practice and public service. Of course, the inevitable, irresistible pun has circulated widely on campus that it took Notre Dame a hundred years to achieve a Lawless Law School.

William B. Lawless received his bachelor of laws degree with honors from Notre Dame in 1944. Immediately upon graduation, as a member of the Naval R.O.T.C., he was assigned to the Pacific combat area, and served as a gunnery officer for two years. On leaving the Navy, he became an associate in the law office of Kenefick, Cooke, Mitchell, Bass and Letchworth in Buffalo, and at the same time pursued night studies at the University of Buffalo in history and government, graduating with the degree of bachelor of arts in 1949. In the fall of that year he entered the Harvard Law School from which he received the master of laws in 1950. For the next ten years he divided his time between private practice and public service: trial lawyer in the firm of Williams, Crane and Lawless (1950–1953) and senior partner in the office of Lawless, Offermann, Fallon and Mahoney (1956–1959); Corporation Counsel for the city of Buffalo (1954–1956) and Special Counsel for Governor W. Averell Harriman (1955–1958). In 1960 he became a Justice of the Supreme Court of New York, from which position he resigned in order to come to Notre Dame. The assignments he has filled in public service on local, state and federal levels, and the assignments he has held in the American Bar Association are too many to list in detail. For these services he received recognition through several awards—Buffalo Junior Chamber of Commerce "Man of the Year" (1956), New York Junior Chamber of Commerce "Man of the Year" (1957), Notre Dame "Man of the Year" (1962), and Buffalo Chamber of Commerce "Good Government Award" (1968). In addition to numerous articles in law journals, he co-authored *New York Pattern Jury Charges* (Lawyer's Co-op, 1965. 2 vols.).

It is a platitude that the human condition and indeed all things in the material universe are subject to constant change. But contrary to philosophers from the Greek Heraclitus to Jean-Paul Sartre and the modern prophet of general semantics, Alfred Korzybski, who seriously advocates abolishment of the verb "to be," a permanence remains in the midst of change. And so throughout the first hundred years many changes have taken place in the teaching of law at Notre Dame and in the activities which have supplemented the formal instruction. The greatest changes have quite naturally occurred at the beginning of new administrations, and this continues to be true as Dean Lawless enters upon his administration. A permanence remains, but this chapter will deal only with the changes and the forward thrust of new undertakings.

Some of the changes are striking and, following the topical sequence of preceding chapters, the first of these pertains to the curriculum—the elective system, abolished in the O'Meara era, has been re-instated, although limited to the second and third years. This gives upper classmen the opportunity to concentrate on areas of the law in which they have a particular interest. The prescribed courses adopted for 1969–1970 are: First Year: year courses in Torts, Contracts, Criminal Law, Procedure, Property, and Legal Bibliography (1 hr. each semester); Second Year: another year course in Procedure, and semester courses in Business Associations,

Labor Law, Criminal Law III, Comparative Law, Legal Research and Writing (1 hr.), Constitutional Law, Jurisprudence, Administrative Law, and Evidence; Third Year: another year course in Property, a year course in Practice Court, and semester courses in Federal Income Taxation, Legal Research and Writing (1 hr.), Family Law, and Secured Transactions.[1]

The third-year electives are divided into courses and seminars. The courses are: Antitrust Law, Conflict of Laws, Admiralty, Community Property, Advanced Legal Research, Negotiable Instruments, Tax Planning and Insurance; and the seminars are Commercial Law, Copyright Problems, Social Problems, Air and Space Law, Organized Crime, Legal Counselling, Legal History, and Modern American Jurisprudence.[2]

A development rather than a change seems promised in a stronger emphasis on correlating law study and research with sociology and other disciplines without which many legal problems cannot be fully understood. Thus Dean Lawless has said: "Generally, legal education has concentrated on laws and procedures to train its practitioners. The new trend in law is to provide a research laboratory for our many social problems and to create better relations with the local and state bar associations in an effort to provide more opportunity for our students to confront the real problems they will face in practice." One aspect of this trend is the involvement of students in urban affairs, which was initiated during the O'Meara years. Hence, Dean Lawless continues: "We now have many of our second and third year students actively involved in local legal aid and defender programs. They do basic case work, research, interviews, briefs and, in general, sense where their services will be most needed in the future."[3] And again he has said: "To study criminal law without relating it to sociology, penology and criminology is inadequate for our times. To study municipal law without relating it to the problems of cities, the problems of minority groups and the problems of the poor is inadequate in 20th century America. To study family law without . . . probing the social aspects of family decline is not to understand fully the legal problems in juvenile delinquency. Indeed, to study law without some deep understanding of the moral basis for all law is both futile and hopeless. . . . It is our mission to rise above the new wave of utilitarianism and secularism. It is our hope to provide our students with a unifying vision of the spiritual sources from which Western civilization flowed."[4]

Re-introducing an elective system into the law program and a greater emphasis on correlating law studies with studies in other disciplines are not innovations, but a completely new departure from the past is the Year Abroad Program inaugurated in this centennial year. This program is open to second-year students, and twenty of them are in London this first year, taking a program of courses at the Faculty of Laws of University College, University of London, whose co-operation made the program possible. Their courses include International Law, Jurisprudence, and two elective courses which correspond to the prescribed second-year courses at Notre Dame. The students may also attend classes at the Inns of Court Law School. The year abroad program offers law students unique opportunity to study on a comparative basis the law of the United States and of England, an opportunity which students of no other American law school have. Primary aims of the program, therefore, are first to give the students a broader base or perspective of the law, and to provide for students interested in international and comparative law and for those interested in practicing American law abroad.

In this first year, two members of the Notre Dame law faculty are in residence with the students, Professor Conrad Kellenberg, who has been at Notre Dame since 1956, and Professor George W. Keeton, Fellow of the British Academy, who until recently was head of the Faculty of Laws at University College. These men will teach the students the American aspects of the courses they are following and supplement their study of English law with American materials. In addition, the students have access to an excellent American law library in London at the Institute of Advanced Legal Studies, close by the University College. On successful completion of their year of study, the students will be awarded a Certificate of British and American Law.

A beginning has been made with the twenty students in London this year. Plans call for the continuation of the London program and for establishment of overseas programs in Japan and South America at an early date. Dean Lawless has expressed his enthusiasm for the program and the reason which prompted its inauguration: "Imagine the excitement with which our third year seminars will be conducted when Notre Dame Law students who have studied in England, Japan and South America rejoin their third year class. We don't mean to suggest that we are going to abandon the traditional training in American law for the majority who wish to emphasize it; rather we agree with the founders of the international legal studies at Harvard Law School that the practitioner of the future must understand in a general way, at least, legal systems other than his own."[5]

Other changes planned for the future will be in student enrollment, number of full-time faculty members, expansion of facilities, especially library facilities, and increase in library holdings. But these changes are dependent upon the construction of a new law building —A Notre Dame Law Center. For years Dean O'Meara pleaded in vain for an addition to the present law building to meet urgent needs. Now a new building is to be built. The architect's drawings have been completed, drawings based on his close study of twenty-five modern law school buildings. As planned, the new building will provide space for six hundred students, a minimum of twenty-five faculty offices, offices for the dean, associate and assistant deans, registrar and secretaries, eighteen classrooms including seminar rooms, a research institute, a library with shelf capacity for 160,000 volumes, and lounges for students and faculty. Estimated cost of this new Notre Dame Law Center is three and one half million dollars for construction and one half million for equipment and furnishings. In addition, one million dollars will be allocated for faculty development and one million for law books. This

Artist's Conception of New Law Center

is surely far beyond the wildest dreams of the founders of the law department a century ago.

A student body of six hundred! This is indeed a notable change, the beginning of a truly new era of law at Notre Dame. Once facilities are provided, there seems to be no great difficulty in building up to this number over the next few years. For September 1969, approximately one thousand applications have been received. This greatly increased number of applications is in large part due to intensive recruitment procedures. Recruitment was started at Notre Dame and letters were sent to all juniors and seniors in the colleges of the university who were on a Dean's List; sixty applications were the result of this effort. Then, every member of the faculty spent one week visiting colleges and universities in all parts of the country. And finally, eight students, four black and four white, went to the campuses of twenty-nine institutions in the South. The special objective of these students was to recruit black students, and their efforts were fruitful—one hundred fifty-seven applications from black students of whom forty-seven were admitted and fifteen awarded scholarships. It is now established policy to recruit law students among minority groups, blacks, Mexican-Americans, American Indians, from homes that could not possibly provide the means for a legal education. If this policy is to prove successful several things are necessary. Applications must be carefully screened to assure as far as possible that applicants admitted give promise of being successful in their law studies; it is evident that the applications for September 1969, have been thus screened. In the measure possible, interviews should be held with these applicants. When students are admitted even though their qualifications are somewhat questionable, they must have clear understanding that they will have to take a pre-law school training program (CLEO), and also receive remedial work while in law school, because there can be no lowering of standards for them. And finally, scholarships and other financial aid must be available.

The preceding chapter described in some detail the law school scholarship program and the rapid growth in scholarship funds during the past few years. This has been the most intensive program in the nation; per capita, Notre Dame offers two and a half times more scholarships than does the Harvard Law School. This intensive program will be continued, and in addition a new loan program has been negotiated. In this new program first-year law students will be eligible for loans instead of only the second- and third-year students, and the money that can be borrowed will be twenty-five hundred dollars a year instead of one thousand, as under the previous program. Hence there is good hope that adequate financial assistance will be available for minority groups students and for others in need.

In this centennial year the law faculty numbers fifteen full-time members, one adjunct professor, five lecturers and two librarians, who are part-time members. The goal is to build the faculty to twenty-five full-time members. Two chairs for distinguished professors have thus far been endowed. Dean Vurpillat with his faculty of two full-time men in 1919 was fifty years too early.

When the present law building was built in 1929–1930, the shelf capacity of its library was thirty-five thousand volumes; the projected law center will have a library for one hundred sixty thousand volumes. Space for books and other legal documents will, therefore, be provided and the most urgent problem facing the law school is the strengthening of library holdings as expeditiously as possible. Although library holdings increased in the O'Meara years, they did not increase nearly fast enough, as Dean O'Meara never tired of repeating to the university administration. Today with sixty-nine thousand volumes the law library falls below the basic requirements of the American Bar Association and of the Association of American Law Schools. The latter association has recently upgraded its requirements for law school libraries, but Notre Dame does not meet even the previous requirements. It is no exaggeration to state that continuing accreditation of the Notre Dame Law School could depend on a clear intention to increase library holdings rapidly. In view of this, effort will be made to raise one million dollars for book purchases over the next few years.

In a recent issue of *Time* magazine the writer of the section on law noted that "Early in the 1960's a small number of law schools began to issue [*sic*] the Doctor of Jurisprudence (J.D.) degree instead of the standard Bachelor of Laws (LL.B.). Soon a few holders of the J.D. discovered that they got job offers ahead of LL.Bs. solely on the basis of their impressive sounding degree. The significance was not lost on the American Bar Association, which endorsed the new degree with uncharacteristic haste. . . . Without fanfare more than 109 of the 150 accredited law schools in the United States have now switched."[6] The Notre Dame Law School is among those that made the change, and henceforth the *juris doctor* degree will be conferred in place of the bachelor of laws at the end of the three-year law course. The doctor of jurisprudence, however, is not a new degree at Notre Dame; former Dean Clarence Manion was one of the first to receive it here in 1922, and a *University Bulletin* announcement preceded that by several years: "The degree of Doctor of Laws (J.D.) or Doctor of Civil Law (D.C.L.) presupposes the degree of Bachelor of Laws and the Bachelor's degree in Arts or Science."[7] Then in the *Bulletin* for 1925–1926 appears the statement: "Students entering the College of Law with a bachelor's degree who complete the full program with an average grade of 85% [later raised to 90%], and submit a thesis acceptable to the faculty of the College of Law, may receive the degree of Juris Doctor (J.D.) in place of the degree Bachelor of Laws."[8] In the past, therefore, to be eligible for the J.D. degree required more pre-legal and legal education than did the LL.B. That will no longer be true, and when large numbers of young lawyers are entitled to sign the J.D. after their names, the degree will lose the "status" value which it apparently has at present and will no longer give the advantage which it now does to the few who have received it. Nevertheless as professional degree the doctor of jurisprudence (J.D.) is perhaps preferable to the bachelor of laws (which represents three years of study beyond the college bachelor degree), corresponding as it does to the professional degree of doctor of medicine (M.D.).

The centennial celebration which marked the end of a century of law at Notre Dame and the beginning of a second century was held at the university on February 7 and 8, 1969. It was both an impressive academic event and a gala celebration. Hundreds of law alumni returned to the campus to participate in the events. A symposium on Human Rights and the Law opened on the Friday afternoon and closed Saturday at noon. The topics of its three sessions were: The Moral Basis of Human Rights, The Moral Basis of Violence, and The Moral Basis of Legal Education. An Academic convocation followed the symposium. The convocation address was given by the Honorable William J. Brennan, Jr., Associate Justice of the Supreme Court of the United States, and honorary degrees of Doctor of Laws were conferred on Dean Emeritus Joseph O'Meara and Professor Emeritus William D. Rollinson, who served on the law faculty from 1930 to 1963.

At the law school reunion dinner Friday evening, the Honorable Raymond Broderick, Lieutenent Governor of Pennsylvania and past president of the Notre Dame Law Association, reviewed the highlights of the first hundred years in his talk, "Notre Dame Law School: The Past." At the centennial banquet the next evening, Dean Lawless struck the note of the future, a note of high hopes and great expectations. And James Barba, president of the Student Bar Association, summed up well the Notre Dame Law School of the present as it looks to the years ahead: "Thus as we turn toward a new century, I may confidently report to you that the state of the Law School is one of change, movement, innovation, enthusiasm and firm confidence in the future."

NOTES

1. Of the prescribed courses, a noticeable difference from the prescribed program of the preceding era is that Professional Responsibility is missing. However, a note states that "Professional responsibility is integrated with each law course and a series of lectures on Professional Responsibility is given by the Law Faculty." *Bulletin of the Law School* (1969–70), 27.
2. *Ibid.*, 26–27.
3. *Notre Dame: Insight* (Fall 1968), 14.
4. Much of what is written in this chapter is based on an address delivered by Dean Lawless at the centennial banquet on February 8, 1969 and on the minutes of the spring 1969 meeting of the Advisory Council for the law school.
5. Address delivered at centennial banquet, February 8, 1969.
6. *Time* (April 25, 1969), 63.
7. *University Bulletin* (1908–09), 102.
8. *Ibid.* (1925–26), 170.

APPENDIX 1A

Faculty of Law
1869–1969

Chronological Order
(with beginning and terminal years)

COLOVIN, M. T., LL.B. (1869–70)
FOOTE, PETER, A.M. (1869–71)
MCKINNON,* HON. J. J. (1870–71)
MORAN,* T. A., LL.B. (1870–71)
STANFIELD,* HON. THOMAS, LL.B. (1870–71)
BROWN,* C.S.C., REV. M. B. (1870–71)
TONG, LUCIUS G., M.A., LLB. (1871–72; 1873–82; 1892–98)
BIGELOW, C.S.C., F. C., A.B., M.A., LL.B. (1871–72; 1874–78)
O'CONNELL,* C.S.C., JOHN A. (1874–76)
HOWARD, TIMOTHY E., A.M., LL.B. (1876–81; 1883–85; 1892–1916)
IVERS, W. J., LL.B. (1878–80)
MCGINNIS,* B. J., LL.B. (1880–81)
EDWARDS,* J. F., LL.B. (1880–81)
UNSWORTH, A. C., A.M. (1881–83)
HOYNES, WILLIAM J., A.M., LL.B. (Dean and Professor of Law, 1883–1919; Dean Emeritus, 1919–33)
GIBBONS, JOHN, A.M., LL.B. (1883–97)
YOUNG, FRANK W., LL.B. (1883–84)
EGBERT, ANDREW J., A.M., J.D.U. Göttingen (1884–86)

* Part-time member of faculty or lecturer

EWING, JOHN J., A.M., LL.B. (1884–85; 1892–98)
HUBBARD, HON. LUCIUS, LL.D. (1892–1904)
BRICK, ABRAHAM L., LL.B. (1892–1901)
SCALES,* HON. FRANK, LL.D. (1892–96)
PENDERGAST,* HON. RICHARD (1892–96)
BREEN, WILLIAM P., A.M., LL.B. (1892–98)
CLARKE, GEORGE E., A.M., LL.M. (1892–98)
KIRSCH,* C.S.C., ALEXANDER, (1892–98)
CHAMBERLAIN,* HON. ORVILLE T. (1900–01)
HUBBARD, ARTHUR L., A.M., LL.D. (1900–16)
MURPHY, DANIEL P., A.B., LL.B. (1901–02)
STEELE, SHERMAN, LITT.B., LL.B. (1904–08)
ADAMS,* ANDREW (1904–13)
RENO,* J. B., A.M., LL.B. (1904–07)
SCHUMACKER,* C.S.C., MATTHEW (1904–05)
SCHWABB, EDWARD H., LL.B. (1905–09)
HIGGINS,* EDWARD C., LL.M. (1905–07)
O'NEILL, HUGH, A.M., LL.B. (1905–07)
O'KEEFE, P. J., LL.B. (1906–07)
FARABAUGH, GALLITZAN, A.B., LL.B. (1908–27)
CALLAHAN, JOSEPH, A.M., LL.B. (1910–13)
MCINERNY, WILLIAM, LL.M. (1913–17)
PAM,* MAX (1913–15)
VURPILLAT, FRANCIS J., LITT.B., LL.B. (1915–23, appointed Dean, 1919)
TIERNAN, JOHN, A.B., LL.B. (1915–22)
PETENGILL,* SAMUEL, LL.B. (1916–17)
PLANTE, JOSEPH O., A.B., LL.B. (1919–23)
COSTELLO, JAMES P., LL.B. (1920–21)
FREDERICKSON, EDWIN, LL.B. (1920–28)

HUNTER, ARTHUR, LL.B. (1921–22)
JONES,* VITUS G., LL.B. (1921–22)
PARKER,* SAMUEL, A.B. (1921–22; 1927–28)
WOYWOOD,* O.F.M., STANISLAS (1921–23)
WATERS, DANIEL, LL.B. (1922–24)
KONOP, THOMAS, LL.B. (Dean and Professor of Law, 1923–41; Professor of Law, 1941–49; Dean Emeritus, 1941–64)
BURLEY, WILLIAM, LL.B., J.D. (1923–25)
HEILMAN, RAYMOND J., A.B., LL.M. (1923–24)
MONTGOMERY, CHESTER, A.B., LL.B. (1923–24)
McGOORTY,* HON. JOHN P., A.B., LL.B. (1923–24; 1938–42)
SCANLON,* HON. KICKAM J., LL.D. (1923–24)
WOOTEN, DUDLEY G., A.M., LL.D. (1924–28)
HADLEY, EDWIN W., A.B., J.D. (1924–26)
MANION, CLARENCE, A.M., PH.M., J.D., J.U.D. (1924–52, appointed Dean, 1941)
RICHTER, ELTON, A.M., J.D. (1924–58; Professor Emeritus, 1958–62)
KIRBY, JAMES F., A.M., J.D. (1927–30)
JACKSON,* FRANK M. (1927–28)
McDONALD,* MAJOR CHARLES (1927–28)
WHITMAN, JOHN, A.M., J.D. (Librarian 1925–42; Faculty 1929–42)
HUGUENAND, AARON H., LL.B. (1928–31)
McCABE, L. O., A.B., LL.B. (1928–30)
EARL, HOMER Q., A.B., J.D. (1929–42)
DOHERTY,* C.S.C., PAUL D., LL.B. (1929–31)
DEAHL,* HON. ORLO R., LL.B. (1929–34; 1947–48)

OSCHE,* HON. M. M., LL.B. (1929–32; 1945–48)
CAIN, WILLIAM, LL.B. (1930–38)
ROLLISON, WILLIAM D., A.B., LL.M. (1930–63; Professor Emeritus, 1963–
ROEMER,* WILLIAM F., PH.D. (1936–44)
BROUGHALL,* C.S.C., LAWRENCE V. (1938–44)
KEARNEY, JAMES J., A.B., J.D., LL.M. (1939–42)
LASHBROOK, MRS. LORA, LL.B. (1942–47)
PEAK,* HON. ELMER J. (1943–55)
CAVANAUGH,* C.S.C., JOHN J., A.B. (1945–52)
POUND,* ROSCOE (1945–47)
KILEY,* HON. ROGER, LL.B. (1945–52)
LAWRENCE, MARIE K., A.B., A.B.L.S., M.S. (Librarian, 1945–66)
FEENEY, BERNARD J., A.B., LL.B. (1946–49)
REUSCHLEIN, HAROLD G., A.B., LL.B., J.S.D. (1946–48)
ROBERTS, LOUIS L., A.M., LL.B. (1946–48)
THORNBURG,* JAMES F., A.B., J.D. (1946–48; 1968–69)
CHROUST, ANTON-HERMANN, PH.D., J.U.D., J.S.D. (1946–
DOHENY,* C.S.C., WILLIAM J., A.B., J.U.D. (1946–48)
BRODERICK, JOHN J., A.B., J.D., M.P.A. (1947–
JACKSON,* LOUIS, LL.B. (1947–56)
KNOBLOCK,* EUGENE, LL.B. (1947–54)
SCANLON,* ALFRED L., A.B., LL.M. (1947–51)
SULLIVAN, ROBERT E., A.B., LL.B. (1947–54)
BARRETT, EDWARD, A.M., LL.B. (1947–
MILLER, JACK R., A.M., LL.B. (1948–49)
PREKOWITZ, WILLIAM A., LL.B. (1949–50)
SHEEDY,* C.S.C., CHARLES E., A.B., LL.B., S.T.D. (1949–59)

BURNS,* ROBERT F., A.B., M.S., LL.B. (1950–52)

PETERS, ROGER P., A.B., LL.B., J.D. (1950–

BRODEN, THOMAS F., JR., LL.B., J.D. (1950–

BUCZOWSKI,* JOHN A., PH.B. LL.B. (1952–58; 1965–69)

O'MEARA, JOSEPH, A.B., LL.B. (Dean and Professor of Law, 1952–68; Dean Emeritus, 1968–

WAGNER, W. J., J.D., LL.M., S.J.D. (1953–60)

DEVINE, HUGH W., B.S., M.A., J.D., LL.M. (Research Associate, 1953–54)

HESBURGH,* C.S.C., THEODORE M., PH.B., S.T.D. (1953–57)

WARD, BERNARD J., A.B., LL.B., LL.M. (1954–69)

SWYGERT,* HON. LUTHER M., LL.B. (1954–

LEVY,* NATHAN, A.B., J.D. (1954–59; Adjunct Professor, 1959–62)

FORD, JOHN P., A.B. (Research Assistant, 1954–55)

DELUNA,* ANTONIO, J.D., S.J.D. (Visiting Professor of Natural Law, 1956–57)

KELLENBERG, CONRAD L., A.B., LL.B. (1956–

DEMPSEY,* HON. F. KENNETH, LL.B. (1956–59)

GRANT,* HON. ROBERT A., A.B., LL.B. (1956–58)

MCGOWAN,* GRAHAM W., A.B., LL.B. (1956–58)

RODES, ROBERT E., A.B., LL.B. (1957–

BOARMAN,* C.S.C., GLEN R., A.B., M.A. (1957–60)

KRASNOWIECKI, JAN, B.A., M.A., B.C.L., LL.M. (1958–60)

BRADLEY,* FRANCIS X., B.S., M.S., J.D., LL.M. (1958–61)

BERNARD,* C.S.C., GEORGE, A.B., S.T.L., S.T.D. (1959–60)

WOFFORD, HARRIS, JR., B.A., LL.B. (1960–66)

ROPER,* JOSEPH A., A.B., LL.B. (1960–61)

SWEENEY,* C.S.C., ROBERT H., A.B., LL.B., J.C.L. (1960–66)

NOONAN, JOHN T., M.A., PH.D., LL.B. (1962–68)

BOYNTON,* CHARLES M., A.B., J.D. (1962–

ROMEO,* VINCENT J., B.S., LL.B. (1962–69)

KERTESZ,* STEPHEN, J.U.D. (1963–66)

SHAFFER, THOMAS L., A.B., J.D. (1964–

BLAKEY, G. ROBERT, A.B., LL.B. (1965–

LEWERS, C.S.C., WILLIAM M., A.B., J.D. (1965–

FARMANN, KATHLEEN G., A.B., LL.B., J.D., M.L.L. (Librarian, 1966–

FARMANN, STANLEY L., A.B., M.S.L.S. (Assistant Librarian, 1966–

CAREY,* JOHN L., B.S.C., J.D., LL.M. (1968–

GRAY, EDWARD J., B.S., LL.B. (Visiting Professor, 1968–69)

O'BRIEN, LEO J., A.B., J.D., LL.M. (1968–69)

THORNTON, PETER W., A.B., LL.B. (Visiting Professor, 1968–69; Professor, 1969–

BOOKER, FRANK E., LL.B. (1969–

FASCHIO, LESLIE G., B.A., LL.B. (1969–

HENRY, GODFREY, B.A., J.D. (1969–

MURDOCK, CHARLES W., B.S., J.D. (1969–

RICE, CHARLES E., A.B., LL.B., LL.M., J.S.D. (1969–

CLEVELAND, GRANVILLE, B.S. (Library Staff, 1969–

APPENDIX 1B

Faculty of Law
1869–1969

Alphabetical Order
(with beginning and terminal years)

ANDERSON,* ANDREW (1904–13)

BARRETT, EDWARD, A.M., LL.B. (1947–

BERNARD,* C.S.C., GEORGE, A.B., S.T.L., S.T.D. (1959–60)

BIGELOW, C.S.C., F. C., A.B., M.A., LL.B. (1871–72; 1874–78)

BLAKEY, G. ROBERT, A.B., LL.B., (1964–

BOARMAN,* C.S.C., GLEN R., A.B., M.A. (1957–60)

BOOKER, FRANK E., LL.B. (1969–

BOYNTON,* CHARLES M., A.B., J.D. (1962–

BRADLEY,* FRANCIS X., B.S., M.S., J.D., LL.M. (1958–61)

BREEN, WILLIAM P., A.M., LL.B. (1892–98)

BRICK, ABRAHAM L., LL.B. (1892–1901)

BRODEN, THOMAS F., JR., LL.B., J.D. (1950–

BRODERICK, JOHN, JR., A.B., LL.B. (1947–

BROUGHALL,* C.S.C., LAWRENCE V. (1938–44)

BROWN,* C.S.C., M. B. (1870–71)

BUCZOWSKI,* JOHN A., PH.B. LL.B. (1952–58; 1965–69)

BURLEY, WILLIAM, LL.B., J.D. (1923–25)

BURNS,* ROBERT F., A.B., M.S., LL.B. (1950–52)

CAIN, WILLIAM, LL.B. (1930–38)

CALLAHAN, JOSEPH, A.M., LL.B. (1910–13)

---

* Part-time member of faculty or lecturer

CAREY,* JOHN L., B.S.C., J.D., LL.M. (1968–

CAVANAUGH,* C.S.C., JOHN J., A.B. (1945–52)

CHAMBERLAIN,* HON. ORVILLE T. (1900–01)

CHROUST, ANTON-HERMANN, PH.D., J.U.D., J.S.D. (1946–

CLARKE, GEORGE E., A.M., LL.M. (1892–98)

CLEVELAND, GRANVILLE, B.S. (Library Staff, 1969–

COLOVIN, M. T., LL.B. (1869–70)

COSTELLO, JAMES P., LL.B. (1920–21)

DEAHL,* HON. ORLO R., LL.B. (1929–34; 1947–48)

DELUNA, ANTONIO, J.D., S.J.D. (Visiting Professor of Natural Law, 1956–57)

DEMPSEY,* HON. F. KENNETH, LL.B. (1956–59)

DEVINE, HUGH W., B.S., M.A., J.D., LL.M. (Research Associate, 1953–54)

DOHENY,* C.S.C., WILLIAM J., A.B., J.U.D. (1946–48)

DOHERTY,* C.S.C., PAUL D., LL.B. (1929–31)

EARL, HOMER Q., A.B., J.D. (1929–42)

EDWARDS,* J. F., LL.B. (1881–82)

EGBERT, ANDREW J., A.M., J.D.U. Göttingen (1884–86)

EWING, JOHN G., A.M., LL.B. (1884–85; 1892–98)

FARABAUGH, GALLITZAN, A.B., LL.B. (1908–27)

FARMANN, KATHLEEN G., A.B., LL.B., J.D., M.L.L. (Librarian, 1966–

FARMANN, STANLEY L., A.B., M.S.L.S. (Assistant Librarian, 1966–

FASCHIO, LESLIE G., B.A., LL.B. (1969–

FEENEY, BERNARD J., A.B., LL.B. (1946–49)

FOOTE, PETER, A.M. (1869–71)

FORD, JOHN P., A.B. (Research Assistant, 1954–55)

FREDERICKSON, EDWIN, LL.B. (1920–28)

GIBBONS, JOHN, A.M., LL.B. (1883–97)

GRANT,* HON. ROBERT A., A.B., LL.B. (1956–58)

GRAY,* EDWARD J., B.S., LL.B. (1968–

HADLEY, EDWIN W., A.B., J.D. (1924–26)

HEILMAN, RAYMOND J., A.B., LL.M. (1923–24)

HENRY, GODFREY, B.A., J.D. (1969–

HESBURGH,* C.S.C., THEODORE M., PH.B., S.T.D. (1953–57)

HIGGINS,* EDWARD C., LL.M. (1905–07)

HOWARD, TIMOTHY E., A.M., LL.B. (1876–81; 1883–85; 1892–1916)

HOYNES, WILLIAM J., A.M., LL.B. (Dean and Professor of Law, 1883–1919; Dean Emeritus, 1919–33)

HUBBARD, ARTHUR L., A.M., LL.D. (1900–16)

HUBBARD, HON. LUCIUS, LL.D. (1892–1904)

HUGUENAND, AARON H., LL.B. (1928–31)

HUNTER, ARTHUR, LL.B. (1921–22)

IVERS, W. J., LL.B. (1878–80)

JACKSON,* FRANK, (1927–28)

JACKSON,* LOUIS, LL.B. (1947–56)

JONES,* VITUS G., LL.B. (1921–22)

KEARNEY, JAMES J., A.B., J.D., LL.M. (1939–42)

KELLENBERG, CONRAD L., A.B., LL.B. (1956–

KERTESZ,* STEPHEN, J.U.D. (1963–66)

KILEY,* HON. ROGER, LL.B. (1945–52)

KIRBY, JAMES F., A.M., J.D. (1927–30)

KIRSCH,* C.S.C., ALEXANDER, (1892–98)

KNOBLOCK,* EUGENE, LL.B. (1947–54)

KONOP, THOMAS, LL.B. (Dean and Professor of Law, 1923–41; Professor of Law, 1941–49; Dean Emeritus, 1941–64)

Krasnowiecki, Jan, B.A., M.A., B.C.L., Ll.M. (1958–60)

Lashbrook,* Mrs. Lora, Ll.B. (1942–47)

Lawrence, Marie K., A.B., A.B.L.S., M.S. (Librarian, 1945–66)

Levy,* Nathan, A.B., J.D. (1954–59; Adjunct Professor, 1959–62)

Lewers, C.S.C., William M., A.B., J.D. (1965–

Manion, Clarence, A.M., Ph.M., J.D., J.U.D. (Professor of Law, 1924–41; Dean and Professor of Law, 1941–52; Dean Emeritus, 1952–

Miller, Jack R., A.M., Ll.B. (1948–49)

Montgomery, Chester, A.B., Ll.B. (1923–24)

Moran,* T. A., Ll.B. (1870–71)

Murdock, Charles W., B.S., J.D. (1969–

Murphy, Daniel P., A.B., Ll.B. (1901–02)

Murphy, Edward J., B.S., Ll.B. (1956–

McCabe, L. O., A.B., Ll.B. (1928–30)

McDonald,* Major Charles (1927–28)

McGinnis,* B. J., Ll.B. (1880–81)

McGoorty,* Hon. John P., A.B., Ll.B. (1923–24; 1938–42)

McGowan,* Graham W., A.B., Ll.B. (1956–58)

McInerny, William, Ll.M. (1913–17)

McKinnan,* Hon. J. J. (1870–71)

Noonan, John T., M.A., Ph.D., Ll.B. (1962–69)

O'Brien, Leo J., A.B., J.D., Ll.M. (Visiting Professor, 1969–

O'Connell,* C.S.C., John A. (1874–76)

O'Keefe, P. J., Ll.B. (1906–07)

O'Meara, Joseph, A.B., Ll.B. (Dean and Professor of Law, 1952–68; Dean Emeritus, 1968–

O'Neill, Hugh, A.M., Ll.B. (1905–07)

Osche,* Hon. M. M., Ll.B. (1929–32; 1945–48)

Pam,* Max (1913–15)

Parker,* Samuel, A.B. (1921–22; 1927–28)

Peak,* Hon. Elmer J. (1943–55)

Peters, Roger P., A.B., Ll.B. (1950–

Pettengill,* Samuel, Ll.B. (1916–17)

Plante,* Joseph O., A.B., Ll.B. (1919–23)

Pound,* Roscoe (1945–47)

Prekowitz, William A., Ll.B. (1949–50)

Pendergast,* Hon. Richard (1892–96)

Reno,* J. B., A.M., Ll.B. (1904–07)

Reuschlein, Harold G., A.B., Ll.B., J.S.D. (1946–48)

Rice, Charles E., A.B., Ll.B., Ll.M., J.S.D. (1969–

Richter, Elton, A.M. (1924–62)

Roberts, Louis L., A.M., Ll.B. (1946–48)

Rodes, Robert E., A.B., Ll.B. (1957–

Roemer,* William F., Ph.D. (1936–44)

Rollison, William D., A.B., Ll.M. (1930–63)

Romeo,* Vincent J., B.S., Ll.B. (1962–

Roper,* Joseph A., A.B., Ll.B. (1960–61)

Scales,* Hon. Frank, Ll.D. (1892–96)

Scanlon,* Hon. Kickam J., Ll.D. (1923–24)

Schumacker,* C.S.C., Matthew (1904–05)

Schwabb, Edward H., Ll.B. (1905–09)

Shaffer, Thomas L., A.B., Ll.B. (1964–

Sheedy,* C.S.C., Charles E., A.B., Ll.B., S.T.D. (1949–59)

Stanfield,* Hon. Thomas (1870–71)

Steele, Sherman, Litt.B., Ll.B. (1904–08)

Sullivan, Robert E., A.B., Ll.B. (1947–54)

Sweeney,* C.S.C., Robert H., A.B., Ll.B., J.C.L. (1960–66)

Swygert,* Hon. Luther M., Ll.B. (1954–

Tiernan, John, A.B., Ll.B. (1915–22)

Thornburg,* James T., A.B., J.D. (1946–48; 1968–69)

Thornton, Peter W., A.B., Ll.B. (1969–

Tong, Lucius G., M.A., Ll.B. (1871–72; 1873–82; 1892–98)

Unsworth, A. C., A.M. (1881–83)

Vurpillat, Francis J., Litt.B., Ll.M. (Professor of Law, 1915–19; Dean and Professor of Law, 1919–23)

Wagner, W. J., J.D., Ll.M., S.J.D. (1953–60)

Ward, Bernard J., A.B., Ll.B., Ll.M. (1954–69)

Waters, Daniel, Ll.B. (1922–24)

Whitman, John, A.M., J.D. (Librarian 1925–42; Faculty 1929–42)

Wofford, Harris, Jr., B.A., Ll.B. (1960–66)

Wooten, Dudley G., A.M., Ll.D. (1924–28)

Woywood,* O.F.M., Stanislas (1921–23)

Young, Frank W., Ll.B. (1883–84)

SOURCES

UNPUBLISHED SOURCES:

University of Notre Dame Archives, Hoynes Papers; Vurpillat Papers.

Office of the Vice-President for Academic Affairs, Konop, Manion, and O'Meara Files.

Provincial Archives—Society of Priests, Indiana Province Letters from Timothy E. Howard to Rev. Edward Sorin, C.S.C.; Report of Rev. August Lemonnier, C.S.C., to General Prefect of Studies of the Congregation of Holy Cross.

Office of the Dean of Law

Minutes of Law Faculty Meetings, 1952–1968.

Minutes of Law Advisory Council Meeting, spring, 1969.

Address of Hon. Raymond Broderick, Lieutenant Governor of Pennsylvania at Law School Reunion Dinner, February 7, 1969.

Addresses of William B. Lawless, Dean of the Law School, and of James Barba, President, Student Bar Association, at Centennial Banquet, February 8, 1969.

Office of the Notre Dame Law Association

Minutes of Law Association meetings, 1948 ff.

Letter of Clarence E. Manion to Philip S. Moore, January 30, 1969.

PUBLISHED SOURCES:

Office of Academic Affairs and Notre Dame Collection, Memorial Library.

University Catalogue (1854–1904), *University Bulletin of Information* (1905–1905), *Bulletin of the College of Law* (1946–1954), *Bulletin of the Law School* (1955–).

Notre Dame Law School: Report of the Dean, 1953–1967, Law Library.

Silver Jubilee of the University of Notre Dame, by Joseph A. Lyons. Revised and enlarged edition, Chicago: E. B. Myers and Co., 1869. Notre Dame Collection, Memorial Library.

A Brief History of the University of Notre Dame du Lac, Indiana, 1842–1892. [by Timothy E. Howard] Chicago: The Warner Co., 1895. Notre Dame Collection, Memorial Library.

Colonel Hoynes of Notre Dame, by Thomas A. Lahey, C.S.C. Notre Dame: Ave Maria Press, 1948. Notre Dame Collection, Memorial Library.

Notre Dame: One Hundred Years, by Arthur J. Hope, C.S.C. Notre Dame University Press. Revised edition, 1948.

Notre Dame Law Reporter. Law Library

Notre Dame Lawyer. Law Library

Faculty of the College of Law, 1930 and *University of Notre Dame du Lac, 1934.* Anonymous booklets. Notre Dame Collection, Memorial Library.

Alumnus, publication of the Notre Dame Alumni Association.

Notre Dame: Insight, publication of the Notre Dame Foundation.

Scholastic, student publication of the university.

South Bend News-Times.

South Bend Tribune.

INDEX

*Italicized number indicates that an item is found in a note.